YOU'VE MANAGED L ...I...u, FOUGHT THE POLITICAL FIGHTS, ADAPTED AND COPED, ATTENDED HUNDREDS OF SEMINARS, FORUMS, AND CONFERENCES.

STILL, YOU AIN'T LEARNED NOTHING YET!

With EXTREME MANAGEMENT—the battlefield manual of the Harvard Business School's Advanced Management Program—you will:

• avoid the traps of management by fashion trend

• select a management style that reflects your personality—and stick with it

• learn that pleasing the boss is not Priority One

• tackle the most intimidating chores and expand your powers

• think big by not seeking perfection

• find your comfort zone—then find a way out

• solve a customer problem that wasn't your fault

• become a better manager by taking employee potshots

• look below the deceptively profitable bottom line.

"THE TITLE PROMISES EXTREMES. BOOK AND AUTHOR DELIVER. Practical, accessible, and nearly jargon free.... Stevens's style is ideal for this top-line presentation of AMP's lessons, and he makes deft use of case studies, anecdotes, and personal insights from past participants."

—*Miami Herald*

EXTREME
Management

What They Teach at Harvard Business School's

Advanced Management Program

MARK STEVENS

Published by Warner Books

An AOL Time Warner Company

This book is not a product of the Harvard Business School. Although the School assisted the author in gaining access to faculty and participants, the opinions and conclusions expressed in the book are strictly those of the author and are not in any way endorsed by the Harvard Business School. The author believes and hopes the book accurately portrays the Advanced Management Program.

Warner Books, Inc., 1271 Avenue of the Americas, New York, NY 10020

Visit our Web site at www.twbookmark.com.

 An AOL Time Warner Company

Printed in the United States of America

Originally published in hardcover by Warner Books, Inc.
First Trade Printing: March 2002
10 9 8 7 6 5 4 3 2 1

The Library of Congress has cataloged the hardcover edition as follows:
Stevens, Mark
    Extreme management : what they teach at Harvard Business School's Advanced Management Program / Mark Stevens.
        p. cm.
    ISBN 0-446-52321-6
        1. Executives—Training of—United States.   2. Management—Study and teaching—United States.   3. Harvard University. Graduate School of Business Administration.   I. Title.

HD30.42.U5 S74 2001
658.4'0071'174461—dc21
                                                            00-047744

ISBN: 0-446-67829-5 (pbk.)

Cover design by Tom Tafuri

To Carol Ann
An extreme friend

CONTENTS

Contents

Contents

Mark Stevens

"I like to race sailboats out of Marblehead Harbor. Every time I go out on the water, I am struck by the fact that we all race the same boats with the same number of crew in the same weather conditions. But one crew always manages to outrace the other crew and win. Why? Because their captain understands that the ability to lead and inspire a team makes the pivotal difference in sailing . . . and the same is true in managing."

—Harvard Advanced Management Program Professor Emeritus Robert H. Hayes

PROLOGUE

As the CEO of a marketing company, I spend my days assisting senior managers struggling with issues of leadership. I constantly strategize: how to outmaneuver competitors, how to gain market share, how to develop powerful new offerings that command attention in the marketplace, how to forge effective teams to accomplish these and other critical objectives.

Through the years, I have witnessed some of the best business minds in action—chief executives, corporate raiders, financiers, and entrepreneurs—and I have worked with them in their quest to achieve greater growth, profitability, and shareholder value through innovation, market domination, and operating excellence. Time and again, the ability of these individuals to focus brute intellectual power on real-world business issues and to transform this intelligence into highly effective strategies and tactics has impressed me. They are often able to achieve success within a set of circumstances that appear untenable and unforgiving.

But other times, they come up short, unable to achieve their goals in spite of enormous investments in time, capital, and people. Due to a lack of knowledge, experience, or insight they simply fail to win in instances when a smarter strategy or a deeper understanding would have proven victorious.

This led me to wonder: Is there a place where the corporate elite can gain exposure to creative management concepts and principles that would lead them to a higher level of excellence and success? And could these lessons be utilized by everyone in business, regardless of their experience, rank, or title?

I envisioned a Top Gun School, where a handpicked cadre of senior managers would be immersed in an intensive learning experience that would propel them—and others who would share in their learning—to achieve consistent superiority in the complex and competitive theaters of corporate war. And I imagined gaining access to this learning—from those who taught it and those who absorbed it—and revealing it to anyone seeking to gain an advantage in their personal and professional lives.

Ultimately, I found more than I could have ever hoped. Deep within the Harvard Business School—operating behind its broader and better-known MBA program—is a unique corporate training regimen officially known as the Advanced Management Program (AMP). Launched at the outset of World War II, it was designed to help U.S. industry play a key role in defeating the Nazi blitzkrieg. To date, AMP has quietly shaped the careers of leading executives and their companies for more than a half century. Although well known and highly regarded by the corporate elite—who know it, among other things, as the launching pad for Robert S. McNamara's ascent from AMP instructor to the head of Ford Motor Company to secretary of defense—it has remained a well-kept secret among the general corporate community.

This book will reveal the secrets of AMP—making the knowledge, the methodologies, and the way of thinking the program imparts to a relative few widely available to all who are interested in continuous learning and self-improvement.

As I set out on this course, I was determined to identify the lessons and insights that the faculty and students found the most compelling and valuable in the real world. I wanted the reader to take a virtual seat in the AMP classroom and share the experience of attending the program. In the process I have condensed what is ordinarily a nine-week, $44,000 regimen into a crash course that can be absorbed in the space of an airplane flight and then kept as a desktop guide for meeting and mastering the challenges of corporate competition. Although the book certainly cannot duplicate the experience of meeting and working with peers in a classroom setting, or interacting with the Harvard faculty, it will open a world of knowledge to those who may never be fortunate enough to be recruited to attend the Advanced Management Program by their employers.

My gratitude goes out to the AMP faculty and students who shared their insights and experiences with me, and to the Harvard Business School. Whenever possible I cite the person interviewed but in certain cases I honor the request for anonymity. However, the opinions and conclusions expressed in the book reflect the thinking of the author and his sources—not Harvard Business School.

INTRODUCTION: A HISTORY OF THE ADVANCED MANAGEMENT PROGRAM

The Advanced Management Program can trace its roots back to 1939. In that momentous year, Robert Gueiroard, the son of a wealthy French publishing family, was deep into his MBA training at Harvard Business School. He assumed his days spent absorbing the intricacies of double entry bookkeeping, push-pull marketing, and the principles of corporate leadership on Harvard's bucolic campus would be just one glorious chapter in his life before he would transition into the privileged world of his family's business. But his days at the university were numbered.

Robert Gueiroard's life was redirected by the forces of history on September 1, 1939, when the Nazi threat turned to aggression and 1.5 million German troops, six panzer and four motorized divisions, and 1,600 state-of-the-art aircraft swarmed into Poland. Two days later Britain and France declared war on Germany. As Hitler set his crosshairs on France, Gueiroard was ordered by his government to return home and take up ranks with a French tank corps headed for the front. In an abrupt, disorienting change of lifestyle, Gueiroard moved from the intellectual preserve of Boston, Massachusetts, to the nightmarish violence of the battlefield. Gueiroard's elite unit was equipped with the best French military technology but was swiftly decimated by the Germans.

Although Gueiroard survived the Battle of France, the devastation of his fellow soldiers, his unit, and his country left a deep impression on the young officer and businessman-in-training. After the French were defeated, Gueiroard sought to resurrect his private life. He returned to Harvard but this time armed with a cautionary message for his American classmates. Writing an article in the school's alumni magazine titled "Blitzkrieg Tactics: A Warning to the United States," Gueiroard sounded an alarm that America's historic isolationist position could not hold up in a rapidly shrinking world. He issued a challenge that would have industrial as well as military implications: Could the United States match the German might, tank for tank, fighter plane for fighter plane, bomb for bomb, tactic for tactic, strategy for strategy?

Embedded in Gueiroard's warning was a disturbing message that the nature of warfare was being reinvented by the Nazis in a way that made all previous combat tactics and strategies outdated and highly vulnerable in the face of the German onslaught. For the United States to prevail, it would have to match German might on the battlefield.

"The best way and the only way to stop tank divisions is to use a larger tank division," Gueiroard wrote, "and the only effective active defense against a plane is another plane. If the Germans had no such superiority in the air, our troops would not have been submitted to such continuous destruction. . . .

". . . I wonder whether the people of this country are ready to accept the sacrifices which are required, if this country is to be saved?"*

Gueiroard's question assumed increasing urgency as the Nazi machine rolled across Europe. Stunned by France's humiliating defeat, the United States began to quickly expand its military operation. As the nation assessed its ability to confront and halt the Nazi march, the American industrial sector—which had little experience in serving the extraordinary wartime demands for armament—loomed as the weak link. If the Americans were to win the war, this would have to change.

President Franklin Roosevelt set the pace in early 1940, when he announced a national goal of producing 50,000 airplanes a year. At the time, the aviation industry was pressing to meet a congressional mandate to produce 5,500 planes annually. Considering that only 46,000 planes had been produced in total in the two decades following the end of World War I, Roosevelt's quota seemed impossible.

But as Assistant Secretary of War Louis Johnson made it clear in a speech to the Harvard Business School Alumni Association, the impossible would have to become the possible. "Will any intelligent, patriotic American tell me," Johnson asked, "that we in

*Quoted passages in this section are from *A Delicate Experiment: The Harvard Business School 1908–1945,* by Jeffrey Cruikshank, Boston: Harvard Business School Press, 1987.

the United States cannot equal Germany's effort?" Germany was already turning out four thousand planes per month and plans called for raising that output to six thousand. In this context, Roosevelt's quota appeared essential if Germany was to be defeated.

As daunting as the challenge appeared at the time, history indicated that America could rise to the occasion. The United States had entered the First World War with fifty-five airplanes and thirty-five pilots. By the time that war ended, the nation's air forces totaled 22,000 planes and 35,000 pilots. The precedent of engaging in a global war with minimal resources and emerging as a military powerhouse was established. But this time, the Nazi war machine raised the bar on the challenge and the risks associated with it.

It was in this context that Secretary Johnson issued a warning: "It is my firm conviction, . . . the safety of this country is indeed in jeopardy. . . . Air forces have proven themselves in recent months to be controlling factors in the fortunes of war; and the fortunes of war, at the present stage of civilization, determine the freedom of nations."

For the United States to prevail, an elite corps of business and military leaders needed to be trained to serve as strategic partners with the military. Anything less would cripple America's response to the Nazi threat.

In times of crisis such as this, visionary leaders must take brave, innovative actions, often violating the prevailing rules and precedents. So it was in the fall of 1940 that Harvard Business School dean Wallace Brett Donham took a major step. The school hoped to produce a new breed of business leader capable of providing powerful support to the war effort by introducing two war-related regimens: Industrial Mobilization and Economic Problems of National Defense. Both were created in response to the key question: Could Harvard Business School develop new courses designed specifically to address the business logistics—primarily defense-related production and procurement—of fighting a war? As far as Donham and much of the faculty were concerned, the answer was yes.

The new programs would become incorporated in a twelve-month course, Training for Defense Industries—which was later to be known as War Training at the Harvard Business School. Harvard Business School identified the purpose of the course this way:

"This country is confronted with a shortage of men trained in industrial administration and management. To help fill this need and accelerate its contribution to the national defense effort, the school is offering this twelve-month National Defense Plan for the duration of the emergency."

During this period the U.S. government's Division of Information–Office of Emergency Management launched a national public relations program, Give 'Em Both Barrels. The campaign stressed the importance of linking the military and industrial sectors in a combined assault on behalf of the war effort.

Harvard was positioning itself as the nexus for a new breed of can-do American—a military-corporate warrior capable of delivering a stunning competitive advantage on the world war battlefield. Harvard would assist the armed forces in developing new strategic and tactical skills that would enhance the war effort by training businessmen to help create a more productive and effective private sector as an indispensable partner in mounting a successful campaign to defeat the enemy.

Harvard's contribution would be multifaceted. In June 1941, the Army Air Forces was created as a centralized air combat entity designed to facilitate chain-of-command issues in an increasingly large and complex flying force. AAF chief General Henry H. "Hap" Arnold tapped Harvard to establish a new curriculum focused on statistics. The course was designed to guide air force decision-makers in diagnosing the wide range of scenarios they might face on the front lines, and how to take prompt and effective action.

As the AAF's officers-in-training arrived at Harvard, in June, they were introduced to a powerful lesson: Not only were erroneous statistics dangerous, but accurate statistics applied erroneously could be equally dangerous. This was illustrated by Harvard's legendary case of the Umpteenth Fighter Squadron.

Early in the war two business school researchers visited a small air force base where a fighter squadron shared responsibility for keeping planes aloft at all times over the Roosevelt estate in Hyde Park, New York. The squadron commander at the base assured the Harvard researchers, just as he had assured Washington military officials, that he had thirty planes which could "fly, fight, and bomb" on a moment's notice. His analysis was based on the reports of crew chiefs who made their individual estimates assuming they had unlimited access to a limited common inventory of crew and equipment. But this was a fallacy, since no two planes could share a pilot, a propeller, or a weapon. In fact, the researchers discovered that the squadron commander at any one point in time had only a single plane he could depend upon to "fly, fight, and bomb."

The Harvard Business School program helped develop a new AAF statistical control system that had a powerful impact on the war effort.

"Through a system of new and modified reports, new types of information were generated. A much improved daily report on aircraft status, for example— the so-called 110 report—enabled strategists to know with great precision which planes could indeed 'fly, fight, and bomb.'" (This model of statistical control, furthermore, was adopted after the war by numerous companies. Perhaps the best-known example is the Ford Motor Company, which employed former Stat School researcher and faculty member Robert S. McNamara in precisely this capacity.)

From the outset, the leaders of Harvard's War Training program recognized the need to simulate the impact of war and the threat it posed to the nation. This imbued the participants with the realization that although they were preparing for a new kind of corporate battle on a college campus, the threat they were protecting the nation from was real and immediate.

As part of its war-related efforts, Harvard Business School launched a program designed to retrain experienced business executives to make the conversion from peacetime to wartime employment. The course opened its doors to 121 men between the ages of thirty-five and sixty. All were subjected to an intensive fifteen-week program designed to make them essential components of the war effort by providing them with a strong production background and a working knowledge of finance and organization structures.

This course of study served as a foundation for the elite training program that was emerging on the Harvard campus. Unlike business school curricula, which were either function-specific or broad-based and philosophic, the program provided a holistic view of the management function fused with a pragmatic, hands-on, results-driven orientation.

This approach dovetailed with the work of the War Manpower Commission, a governmental agency whose mandate was to make sure there were sufficient workers in the important war industries. The commission sanctioned Harvard's War Production Training. And chairman Paul McNutt described the course this way:

"With its broad curriculum and objectives, its supervised study, and case method of presentation, it is nowhere duplicated in the country. Never has the country needed administrative talent with a broadened outlook more than now."

"Broadened" is the key word. From the very beginning, Harvard's training was designed to expand perspectives by exposing participants to issues, challenges, and solutions beyond the limited skill sets, knowledge base, and ambitions they brought with them into the course. As Harvard professor Franklin Folts put it, "They are shaken out of grooves." The 1943 summer issue of *Modern Industry* magazine reflected this theme, noting that graduates gained an airplane view of business—an overall view that might otherwise take them years to acquire.

The War Training program at Harvard created an elite class of business managers with knowledge of providing war matériel and a strategy for winning under the most severe conditions. In the aftermath of the war, both Harvard and the business community recognized the enduring value of a high-caliber training regimen that would create an executive brain trust and keep participating companies at the vanguard of free enterprise.

In September 1945, a class of forty candidates—including fifteen demobilized veterans and five entrepreneurs—entered the newly christened Advanced Management Program. A new era in peacetime managerial training had begun.

THE PRINCIPLES OF THE ADVANCED MANAGEMENT PROGRAM

The Advanced Management Program has always been guided by the principle that the academic could be fused with the pragmatic to create a well-rounded and enlightened breed of leaders.

The tactics and methodologies born during the early days of the program have been sharpened and refined through the years to become a field guide for today's business leaders seeking to gain a competitive advantage in global markets. Every spring and fall, selected students descend on the Harvard campus to engage in an exceptional combat school. They are dispatched there by prestigious global companies who pay the tuition to have their handpicked senior managers schooled in the best practices of the best companies as taught by the best professors and enriched by sharing the experience with one's peers. It's an intense program in which core beliefs are brought into question and the workaday world is left behind in pursuit of deeper truths and more effective management practices.

Inside this privileged environment, participants learn to break out of their narrow functions and to understand and acquire new competencies and perspectives. The program highlights five skill sets that focus on the pragmatic application of the curriculum to real-world business issues:

- Making decisions and motivating people.
- Assuring organizational competence.
- Competing successfully in the global arena.
- Improving quality, productivity, and teamwork.
- Understanding modern corporate finance.

The Advanced Management Program also emphasizes these three pillars of managerial excellence:

1. *Despecialization.* Managers must look beyond the micro issues and achieve powerful synergies by integrating the specialized skills and experiences of their team members. The AMP participant is taught to lead a mission that encompasses a broad range of disciplines and functional capabilities. When this goal is achieved, the company and the individual win.

2. *Externalization.* All too many managers are internally focused, taking a myopic view of the world that rarely extends beyond the limited sphere of their day-to-day responsibilities. It's as if they believe they can ignore the forces operating outside their vertical industry position—forces that in one

way or another have a major impact on their business. Whether it's unions, environmentalists, industry regulators, or foreign governments—they try to ignore it all. This blinders-on approach prevents these executives from joining the ranks of the managerial elite. AMP teaches managers creative solutions for achieving business objectives in collaboration with the full range of external forces.

3. *Leadership.* The best leaders recognize that what they know pales in comparison to what they still need to learn. Because they are open to ideas, insights, and revelations that can lead to better ways of accomplishing goals, the best leaders engage in a constant dialogue with advisers, employees, vendors, consultants, and competitors. This communication is designed to make them more proficient in pursuing and achieving objectives. At AMP, this is called the voyage of discovery, as executives learn how to take the steps en route to becoming the best managers in the world.

Armed with these skill sets, fresh perspectives, and knowledge imparted at AMP, attendees can confidently and competently assume the leadership of a corporate department, business unit, or company.

"When the president of Ashland Oil nominated me to attend AMP, I knew it was considered a rite of passage for people on the way up at the company," recalls Phillip Ashkettle. "I was then an Ashland group vice president and my boss and his boss and his boss's boss were all AMP graduates, so I wasn't about to decline the invitation. But I thought it was just another corporate requirement that I could put behind me and say 'been there, done that.'

"But it turned out to be one of the most important learning experiences in my life. I say that from two perspectives. I gained extraordinary insights into effective management- and business-building techniques. And from a career perspective, I came to realize that I could run an entire business—become a CEO—and do so on an accelerated timetable.

"Before the AMP learning experience, I was more or less content to wait my turn rising through the highest echelons of the company. But after AMP, I decided to push the pedal to the floor. The knowledge I gained gave me the confidence to raise the bar on my ambitions and expectations. And it was only three years later that I was recruited to become CEO of Reichold Chemicals, a billion-dollar global company.

"There's no doubt in my mind that AMP helped me get to the top and to improve my performance in my current position. So many of the things I learned at AMP proved to have great practical value. For example, for the first time I was able to look at information technology with a real business perspective. Before AMP training, I viewed it as just a way to gather data and get the numbers into a reporting system. But AMP taught me that a company could use the levers of information technology to create sustainable differentiation in the marketplace.

"At Reichold, I've applied this insight to remake the company's organizational structure. When I arrived here, I found a deep hierarchical structure that bogged the business down across the board. Using information technology as a means of linking people and functions, I dismantled the company's four operating divisions, replacing them with a series of business teams—all with a single layer of management reporting to team leaders and with access to the company's collective resources. This has created operating units that are as close to entrepreneurial companies as you can find in a billion-dollar corporation."

AMP also served as a springboard for Moshe Levy, a former commander in the Israeli army, now CEO of Safeguards Technologies, a producer of security systems that protect such sensitive facilities as Camp David and Buckingham Palace.

"AMP prompts you to think of ways to keep raising the standard on your performance, on the challenges you tackle, and on your ability to succeed," says Levy. "At Harvard, I came in contact with world-class entrepreneurs as well as business executives. Based on the AMP experience, I started to believe that I too could run a major company. So immediately after leaving Harvard, I set out to buy Safeguards Technologies, then a subsidiary of a U.K.-based conglomerate.

"It's important to understand that AMP is motivational as well as informational. The program teaches that once you decide to do something in life, you can accomplish anything. So less than a year after I decided to acquire Safeguards, I structured a leveraged buyout that gave me ownership of the company with only a modest cash investment. In short, AMP helped me to see the possibilities."

The Advanced Management Program is real-world focused. It is based on a living and evolving curriculum of experience gained in the crucible of the marketplace, the financial markets, the legislative arena, and the executive suite. Developed and taught by a distinguished business faculty—with input and guest lectures by prominent corporate executives—AMP training is designed to teach the strategies and tactics for victory in today's global theaters of corporate war and for winning internal corporate battles with peers, ambitious upstarts, and superiors. All of this is valuable for every business executive, at every stage of the career path.

"Before attending AMP, I was in search of a scientific model for managing," says former AT&T vice president and current president and COO of Metrus Group, Inc., Kathryn Anderson. "Think of it as an algorithm that would provide all the answers in a neat and concise way. The problem is, that precision model doesn't exist. Instead, you have to respond to the myriad of issues business throws at you with a combination of art and science, bringing different skills and sensitivities to each set of challenges and opportunities. AMP made me see this, and, equally important, gave me the courage to manage without the security blanket of a fixed methodology."

ABOUT THIS BOOK

This book is a crystallization of the Advanced Management Program, fused with the insights, epiphanies, and strategies of the students who apply the lessons learned there to gain a competitive advantage for their companies and their careers. This dual perspective reflects the fact that AMP is not a static curriculum, but is instead a dynamic experience shaped in part by the executives who participate in its classroom discussions, study groups, and brainstorming sessions. The book reflects the free flow of information from faculty to students, students to faculty, and students to their corporate peers. This cross-pollination captures the richness and vitality of the program as well as the tangible benefits that flow from it.

Currently, AMP students devote nine weeks to the program. In all likelihood, you cannot or will not be selected by your employer to make this kind of extensive commitment away from the front lines of your career. For this reason, we have taken the best of what AMP has to offer and condensed it in a volume you can use immediately.

Extreme Management is divided into five major areas (which cover the major skill sets required to manage effectively) and subdivided into concise sections (which succinctly communicate some of the most compelling and pragmatic lessons). You will find profiles, interviews, lists, and case histories. You can immerse yourself in the AMP experience at any place in the book. How you tackle the program is up to you. It is designed so that you will find practical value every time you pick it up.

The curriculum is not composed of complex scientific principles. Instead, it is a mix of new insights, evergreen ideas updated for immediate application, and creative flashes that can help you change the way you look at your business. Your competitors. Your staff. Your career.

And your role as a manager. Leader. Prospective CEO.

As a vice president of a global communications company put it: "With what I learned, and what I contributed, I felt capable for the first time of running with the top horses."

THE INNER SANCTUM: BEHIND THE CURTAIN OF THE ADVANCED MANAGEMENT PROGRAM

Only a few privileged managers experience the power and personal enrichment of Harvard's Advanced Management Program firsthand. Although you may never be fortunate enough to attend the school, this book will help you expand your horizons and capabilities by sharing some of the most compelling insights of the Harvard faculty and some of their most illustrious students.

As you prepare to immerse yourself in this book, and the highly personal and unique view of AMP that it presents, it will be helpful to see how the program unfolds.

By and large, the AMP regimen is a return to academic life. As participants—most of whom are accustomed to the luxurious lifestyles their careers afford them—arrive on campus, they are assigned to rooms at Harvard Business School's McArthur Hall. Living quarters are structured in suites of eight individual rooms clustered around common areas designed to facilitate group interaction.

Students attend classes six days a week and work for an average of fourteen hours a day. They are expected to be free of personal diversions, to shift their corporate responsibilities to others, and to leave their families at home. In other words, welcome to the world of Extreme Management.

The goal is to refocus businesspeople from a preoccupation with making decisions to an intensive learning experience that prepares them to return to the decision-making role with greater wisdom, knowledge, and perspective.

THE ADVANCED MANAGEMENT PROGRAM REGIMEN

Weeks One and Two

Students are encouraged to think through the management challenges and opportunities they face in their corporate lives and to use this grounding as a means of prioritizing their personal goals and objectives.

Reflecting the AMP focus on developing broad-based management perspectives, students are challenged to move out of their functional silos by exploring a case history of an established company's evolution from a modest domestic player into a global powerhouse. This case demonstrates how a multitude of variables align to create change and how the company is impacted by it.

This opening phase of the program also includes an optional session on the fundamentals of accounting and finance.

Weeks Three Through Eight

This period represents the core of the program, during which students are engaged in an eclectic mix of courses structured to strengthen and embellish their managerial capabilities.

Weeks Nine and Ten

The regimen returns to a wide-angle perspective, integrating the course material into a holistic view of the managerial process. Students gain insights into the responsibilities of the CEO, the senior management team, and the board of directors.

In this phase the program also examines such topics as privatization, corporate renewal, the environment, global alliances and the impact of information technology on management, and competitive advantage. All of this is incorporated in integrated case studies that bring a sense of immediacy and urgency to the course material.

Conclusion of the Program

The faculty assists AMP graduates in planning their reentry to the corporate world. The focus is on using the knowledge and skills they have gained to confront the issues waiting for them on the job.

A TYPICAL DAY IN THE LIFE OF AN ADVANCED MANAGEMENT PROGRAM STUDENT

7:00: Breakfast discussion at Kresge Hall.

8:00: Students meet with their assigned discussion groups to review issues identified during case study preparations.

9:15: Class session. In the Competition and Strategy course the faculty presents insights into Disney's European expansion and the strategic impact of this move on the company.

10:30: Coffee break.

10:50: In the Information, Organization, and Control Systems course the faculty instructor profiles the Singapore TradeNet as a means of demonstrating how information technology can change the competitiveness of a country.

12:00: Lunch at the Kresge Hall Faculty Club.

1:15: Class sessions resume. In the Managing Organizational Effectiveness course faculty and students discuss a realignment of Apple Computer's organization and culture to address evolving realities of the marketplace.

2:30: Free time period during which students take elective courses, attend presentations by guest speakers, work independently or with study groups.

6:30: Dinner and group discussions at the Kresge Hall Faculty Club.

8:00: Students engage in the intensive reading and preparation required for the next day's classes and discussions.

Throughout this academic regimen the Harvard case study method is augmented with the AMP applied learning approach that addresses the real-world issues germane to each participant's career and business management responsibilities. To facilitate this unique blend of classroom and marketplace focus, students are advised to maintain a daily diary that identifies and captures the take-home value from each class or exercise and to reflect on how it can be applied on the job. (I suggest you adopt a similar approach when trying to transfer these lessons into your professional life.)

1

FIRST STRIKE LEADERSHIP:
Mastering the Art and Science of Making Decisions and Motivating People

Throughout my career as an adviser to senior corporate management, I have always focused on the challenges of leadership. That's because I learned early on that strong leadership is imperative for shaping a group of people into a force that serves as a competitive business advantage. The best-performing departments, operating units, divisions, teams, and companies are guided by leaders who understand how to make people function in a collaborative fashion. These leaders also know how to mold them into teams and how to motivate them to exceed the level of performance they would reach under the guidance of less masterful hands.

I have discovered that there is a direct correlation between the way people view their managers and the way they perform. In nearly every case, effective leaders are virtually idolized by the people they lead. Not for their touchy-feely traits, but as men and women willing to wade into the most troublesome, perplexing, and sometimes frightening situations at the head of the pack. These are managers who are willing to take the heat, accept risks, and make difficult decisions under fire. This courage, smarts, savvy, and decisiveness impresses people, inspires confidence, and ultimately makes them want to follow. When this powerful dynamic is in place, the company's resources are marshaled to accomplish its key goals. Results are achieved. Competitors suffer. The business grows.

As is the case for the entire AMP regimen, the insights for making this happen come from the faculty (who have studied the DNA of great leadership in hundreds of companies and offer the wisdom of their discoveries) and from the students (who have proven themselves as effective leaders in the crucible of the marketplace).

Pay close attention to the AMP material, class discussions, personal exercises, and group dynamics and you come away with a formula for successful leadership. You discover that the best decision-makers—the Top Guns in every industry—strike first by taking the offensive against competitors, market trends, and economic cycles. They are skilled at navigating the maze of office politics, competitive forces, and economic roadblocks, and they know how to capitalize on the career-making opportunities that are inherent in every job. First Strike Leadership provides a series of strategic and tactical moves you can use to gain exposure, build credentials, and achieve high-profile successes that resonate with the people you must lead and the superiors who monitor your performance.

For some, the best route to successful leadership is

to identify a role model. When a senior vice president for a large food processor looked into the AMP mirror of self-analysis, she discovered that she was not decisive in making difficult decisions. Concerned that whatever direction she moved in would cause ripples with the CEO and the board, she often reverted to inaction and procrastination just when her smarts and experience were needed most.

This proved more disastrous than making a controversial decision. Absent effective leadership, issues piled up, the staff lacked direction, fear radiated throughout the organization, and competitors filled the vacuum left by the company's failure to act in a timely manner.

It was during an AMP discussion group that the executive heard an anecdote about President Harry Truman. It seemed when Truman had to make one of the most difficult decisions in history—whether or not to drop the atomic bomb on Japan—he struggled with the issue, reviewed the pros and cons, and then gave the military the authorization to proceed. What impressed her most was that once Truman made his decision, he told his adviser Clark Clifford that he promptly retired to his bed, had a sound night's sleep, and never second-guessed himself. As we all know, Truman's decision created a firestorm of controversy that still rages today. But his stature as a decisive leader rests with the fact that he recognized his duty to make difficult decisions regardless of the controversy they would create or the risks they would pose to his popularity. He accepted this as part of the challenge of leadership.

"Faced with the kind of decision that could boomerang on me," the food executive relates, "I used to freeze up, become paralyzed, like a deer in the headlights. The voices in my head drove me batty: What if the CEO thinks this? What if the board does that? Now I realize all of those repercussions may occur, but if I am convinced that I am making the right decision, I can and should have a Truman-like sound night's sleep and never look back. If it turns out I have to reverse myself now and then because my superiors disagree with the course I've taken, that's the price of admission to the executive ranks. And although it's never pleasant to be second-guessed or told you've blundered, the fact that my business and my team are now ahead of the curve, taking options away from competitors because of our speed and decisiveness, is what I focus on. I take my lumps now and then, but we're winning and that's had a very positive impact on my self-esteem and my career."

That's the idea behind First Strike Leadership: to learn new ways of looking at the dynamics of leadership and of leveraging the authority and prerogatives that go with it. Whether you come away from this section with a blueprint for becoming a more decisive, creative, collaborative, visionary, or pragmatic leader, the goal is for you to propel yourself out of the pack and into the upper echelons of your company. Think of it as career coaching from the school— as well as the graduates who have earned their stripes in the corporate sector.

Avoiding the Trap of Management by Fashion Trend

AMP preaches that one of the biggest mistakes a leader can make is to manage by fashion trend. Rather than establishing a managerial style and sticking to it, fickle leaders wander all over the board. They copy others, try on new approaches, and adopt a flavor-of-the-month methodology that leaves everyone thoroughly confused. Even worse, it brands the manager as someone who lacks strength, direction, and focus.

"AMP teaches you to eschew the mix-and-match management style," says a vice president of a global telecommunications company and AMP graduate. "Instead, you learn to look at the practices of great managers and use them as role models. In the process, you come to see that the superb managers select a specific style of management and then invest in it for the long term. This has had a major impact on the way I manage. I used to think that all the great leaders led by intellectual capacity: that they could identify a trend, such as a powerful new technology, and by dint of their genius and foresight get others to follow them. But at AMP, I learned that I didn't have to imitate the quantitative types to be successful. I am strongest on the human, highly personal level—and I can use that strength to lead in a manner that befits me. In fact, another key point that surfaces in the AMP program is that we are all far better managing in ways that complement our personalities, rather than trying to develop leadership styles that run counter to the unique ways we think and act as people."

Armed with the confidence to lead by building collaborative teams, this vice president has built an effective leadership process composed of three key building blocks:

- Strong leadership begins with sound recruitment. Recruit people who will thrive under your management approach.
- Hire people with complementary skills. On one level this is easy. If your team is strong in skills x and y, but deficient in skill z, everyone knows it's important to focus your efforts on filling the z gap. But this becomes more complicated when you are forced to face the fact that the deficiency may rest with you. Although it can be hard to admit that you need others to complement your skills and capabilities, making the admission—and acting on it—is a true test of an enlightened and effective leader.
- Motivating people doesn't mean paying ever-higher salaries. A more powerful approach is to take an interest in your employees. Learn what they want from their jobs and their personal lives and seek to nurture this. If you believe employees desire personal development, for example, be sensitive to this by helping them gain additional education, on-the-job training, and greater responsibility in the company. Your role as mentor and supporter will establish you as a powerful leader.

An interview with a global telecommunications vice president and AMP graduate:

Q. Does your management style shift to reflect changing circumstances?

A. Absolutely. Actually, I would paraphrase someone more famous than me, Colin Powell. I heard him speak a couple of years ago and what he said really rang true: If you're going to be an effective leader, you need to adapt your style and figure out how to work well with the competencies of your team members rather than always expecting that they adapt to you. So I do make changes. But there's only so far I will move. There are times when I say to an employee, it's not right that I change in this circumstance. You've got to change—or leave the team.

Q. What would be your advice to a manager who finds himself in a corporate culture that is hostile to his management style?

A. To leave. I say that based on the experience of finding myself in that situation at one point in my career. Even though I've been inside the same company for twenty-two years, there are very different parts of the company. We're almost like multiple little companies inside the larger company. And once I found myself in a cultural environment that was really hostile. So I went to a couple of people I trusted and I explained to them the situation. I said, I know I can overcome these circumstances. I can work through this. And my confidants looked at me and said, boy are you naive. And ultimately they were right. I think most of us are rooted in an axiom that says "you can always work through it." Maybe my dad believed that, but I have come to a different reality: When faced with such a situation, the smart choice is to vamoose.

Q. Before the AMP program, were you a different kind of manager?

A. Yes. I was a very demanding person. It didn't matter whether I was on the job or at home. My husband would say I was the same way in both places. That I expected the same things. Before AMP, I had a much more in-your-face kind of leadership style. I'd lay it out for people. I expected they'd be able to take the good, the bad, and the ugly. After AMP I changed a lot. I realized that sometimes people couldn't always take that. It may be true but you don't necessarily have to tell them right out. You have to find subtle ways to introduce change, new concepts, and give feedback to people so that they can accept and grow with it. Brutal honesty can even inhibit your career. But my post-AMP management style change didn't happen overnight. I started practicing by targeting a couple of areas where I thought change would be received well. Today, if I were trying to make that kind of change from a very quantitative, hard, report-type person to one a little more humanistic or inspirational, some of the things I might do are: Number one, start with the people who work for you who are already doing fairly well. I have one team that's just knocking the lights out of the numbers. And while they have some challenges to face, they are pretty strong overall. I'd probably start with a team like that, where you can experiment with your style and not screw with their heads. They wouldn't be confused by the signals. Another thing I'd do is find a member of the team

I could confide in. I'd tell him or her, "Here's what I'm trying to do. Help me reinforce this and give me some air cover with the rest of the team." So number two, find a team member who can help you help the rest of the team understand what is going on.

This person's AMP experiences relate to the fact that one can divide the business world into two camps: the street-smart and the quants. The former tend to function on instinct, guts, and experience, the latter on quantitative analysis and spreadsheets.

The quants believe an identifiable management algorithm ties together all the variables of business management and reveals a deep, holistic truth. Their mantra is relatively simple: Find the formula, apply it to a given challenge or opportunity, and success will follow.

But at AMP the students learn that the algorithm is mythical. That the science of management isn't a science at all. Although Kathryn Anderson came to Harvard with a skill set different from that of the telecommunications VP, she left with a similar revelation—and a highly creative way to tackle challenges and opportunities.

"As an engineer by training, with a master's in computer science, I went into AMP thinking that there was a formula for linking all of the variables management must master—quality controls, customer service, supplier negotiations," she says.

"I was pathologically numbers-oriented and believed that in the numbers I would find solutions. But I came out of AMP with a dramatically different perspective. Management, I learned, is more art than science. You can't take given issues—such as expense negotiations, strategy development, and human resources—and seek to solve them scientifically, one at a time. Instead, you have to deal with them holistically, artfully, and with a combination of instinct, analysis, and perspective.

"This revelation changed my management style. Before, I used to ask my staff to create detailed analyses, driving the numbers down to the last decimal point before I felt comfortable enough to make a decision. Now, instead of just using equations to see the light, I find different ways of looking at business issues, problems, and challenges. For example, we might start with a description of a situation and say we want to view it as a dog. Working together, we reshape the image in mind until we feel it reflects the right way to look at and address the problems we're facing together.

"At the early stages of our analysis, we might realize that, for the challenge at hand, we need to be able to look down on the world from a higher vantage point. So we'll give what started out as a dog the neck of a giraffe. Then we may realize that this animal—which is, of course, merely a symbol of our business strategy—will have to endure a severe competitive assault. So we'll give it the protective shell of an armadillo. The process continues until we have visualized a creature that represents all the issues we will likely face and how we intend to face them. Think of it as a creative visioning that takes my team and myself out of the narrow world of numbers and into the expansive universe of concepts and ideas.

"This process is a direct result of my AMP experience, which provided the personal revelation that management is more of gestalt and less of an equation."

PRIVATE LISTS CAN PROVIDE ROAD MAPS FOR MANAGERIAL ACTION

It is human nature for leaders to devote the bulk of their time and energy on the functions, activities, and responsibilities they know and perform best. At first blush, this appears to be a wise division of duties that capitalizes on a manager's strength.

But it's really a trap. With a manager focusing on the components of the business he or she is most comfortable with, components that are painful, confusing, or distasteful suffer from neglect. Bad things keep getting worse. It is only a matter of time before the business unit, and manager responsible for it, faces the day of reckoning.

"We all have private lists of dissatisfactions we experience on the job," says Roy Richards, CEO, Southwire Company (AMP Class of 1994). "Typically, these are the things we know we're not doing well, but that we keep postponing and procrastinating over because there's a personal roadblock in our way: We don't like the issues involved, we feel deficient in dealing with them, or we prefer to focus on the initiatives with the straightest line between action and success. Understandable, but we can't let these preferences serve as a valid excuse for allowing the business unit to sidestep actions that must be taken. Every now and then we have to take the private list out of the locked file and address the issues on it one by one.

"AMP prompts you to seek constant improvement. When I returned from Harvard and looked at my list, I had to admit that I'd become a caretaker manager.

Rather than building a proactive agenda, I was seeking to protect what Southwire had created. AMP made me face the fact that this passive stance would kill us. To change the company's culture and my own leadership style, I knew I needed to be exposed to new voices, challenging voices that would force me out of my comfort zone. To make that happen in a big family business like Southwire, I had to recruit those voices and bring them into our circle. And that leads to another important lesson I learned at AMP: the value of studying excellent leaders, identifying what makes them excellent, and incorporating elements of their approach into your own management style. This led me to move down two significant and interrelated paths.

"First, I searched the corporate world for leaders I admired, and invited them to join our board of directors. Until that point, we'd been a bit insular in our thinking. The introduction of innovative minds helped to widen our perspective as a company and motivated me to tackle the issues on my private list. Second, in studying Hewlett-Packard, Motorola, and other exceptional companies, I discovered that their leaders were not just good at growing sales and profits. They were determined to establish institutional excellence for as long as the company was in business—no matter who is at the helm. When institutional excellence is in place, companies can achieve industry leadership for decades and generations.

"As the CEO of the leading company in the power cable industry, and as the second generation of family stewardship over a $1.7 billion business, I recognized that institutional excellence was the greatest legacy I could leave the company."

GOOD LEADERS REWRITE THE RULES OF THEIR LEADERS

In the brief but compelling history of the computer industry, few episodes are as engaging—and illustrative of a universal truth—as John Sculley's ascent to the leadership of Apple Computer. In a palace revolt that unseated founder and prevailing ruler Steve Jobs, Sculley, the ex-Pepsico marketing executive, was anointed the person who would save the one-time tech wonder company from its insular vision and lack of strong management. For a while it seemed as if Sculley had the magic touch, only to prove—soon enough—that his grand solution for the Apple problem was little more than a short-term fix that could not hold its own in the rapidly changing computer world.

You've read dozens of similar stories. A corporate executive assumes a new position, takes command of a troubled business, extinguishes the fires, and puts the company back on a growth track. With a flourish of ego and pride, he claims victory. The business is fixed. A finely tuned model is in place. Next!

Not quite. One of the key elements of highly effective leadership is the refusal to believe that a business model, however sound and well crafted, is ever good enough to run on autopilot. The fact is nothing is ever truly fixed, finished, or completed because every aspect of business is a work in progress. Recognizing this, the most successful leaders continually improve their models by engaging in a perpetual process of interactive learning.

13

"The great leaders embrace the process of discovery," according to AMP professor emeritus Hugo Uyterhoeven. "Think of it as a perpetual quest for information: asking questions, interviewing, researching, listening to a galaxy of customers, suppliers, professional advisers, peers, superiors, and employees."

AMP graduate Roseanne Antonucci, chief operating officer, the American Woman's Economic Development Corporation (AMP Class of 1991), has found a way to absorb this diverse range of information and use it to shape and enrich her management agenda.

"When I went to work right out of college, the atmosphere was rigid, formal, daunting. Everyone addressed me by my last name. As far as my superiors were concerned, my job was to listen, learn, and do as I was told. No one solicited my opinions and no one would entertain them if I were brash or stupid enough to air them.

"In part, we're all products of what we learn and how we are treated—and I am no exception. So as my career took shape, and my scope of responsibilities expanded to the point that I was managing others, I became aware that I was employing some of the closed-minded tactics others had applied to me. This revelation came to me through AMP's insights on leadership. I realized that every generation of managers must grapple with, and discover, new ways of leading. Because management styles change all the time, it is important to understand that what worked for you when you were looking for someone to lead you is probably not the way you should be trying to lead others in a new era characterized by a completely different business and cultural environment. Basically, good leaders lead by rewriting the rules their leaders led by."

If you want to be a leader, you have to be adaptive. Fresh with this AMP insight, Roseanne Antonucci set out across the country to visit the eight hundred people reporting to her in a previous position. As she drilled beneath the surface of staff-management relationships, she recognized the wisdom of relating to people less as the boss and more as mentor and collaborator.

"When I started out with the corporation I worked for when I participated in the AMP program, I addressed my superiors as Mr. Smith and Mr. Jones," Antonucci recalls. "Later, when I spoke to our CEO, I called him by his first name. That's not because I'd risen to the CEO's level, but because the business environment had evolved—and managers have to change with it. The name issue is just a symbol of something far more powerful and important to the management process: My peers among the baby boomers have to recognize that today's twenty-five-year-old MBAs have to be dealt with differently than we were dealt with at that stage of our careers.

"Assessing the people coming up behind me, I see a self-assured and outspoken staff far better prepared to enter the workplace than my generation had been. They don't want to participate as subordinates only; they want to serve as partners. I encourage them to make recommendations, to pose solutions, and I listen to what they have to say. When I find that their contributions have real merit, we work together to put them into play.

"This has produced a significant return. As people come to recognize that I relate to them on a human level, they relate to me in kind. Behavior is transformed from do what you have to do to please the boss, to see how hard and smart you can work to help achieve the mission."

MICROMANAGERS BEWARE: SELF-PROTECTION IS REALLY SELF-LIMITATION IN DISGUISE

Ambitious executives believe they can rise through the ranks because they are smart, political, aggressive, and driven to avoid mistakes that can blemish their records. To keep the slate clean, they tend to manage people closely, subjecting them to constant scrutiny.

Although this micromanagement can build discipline, it rapidly leads to a point of diminishing returns, because it keeps employees locked within a limited range of actions. Lacking the power to experiment, to take limited risks, or to propose innovations that cannot be fully supported at the outset, micromanaging severely limits the growth of the company and its employees. And so too the manager's company or department. Because the business unit is preoccupied with following the boss's paint-by-numbers formula, it is virtually barred from achieving out-of-the-box accomplishments. The paradox of this management style is that self-protection leads to self-limitation.

Micromanagers clutch the puppet strings because

they believe that lapses in control will lead to dire consequences: unauthorized actions, lack of discipline, renegade policies, departures from the core strategy, and ultimately the failure to achieve growth objectives. But in practice, just the opposite is often true. When micromanagers relax their grip, the organizations reporting to them often flourish because the staff has the opportunity to utilize and demonstrate its full potential. Equally important, the manager has the time, and the mind-set, to engage in broad-based thinking, visioning, and nurturing.

"Post-AMP, I now spend more time thinking about advanced technology and coaching our young engineers instead of micromanaging people," says Dr. Kenneth Rosen, vice president, Sikorsky Aircraft (AMP Class of 1996). "The change has been dramatic. In the past, I walked into meetings using my executive stripes as the symbol of my power. Now I use something even more powerful: my knowledge. In our departmental meetings, I serve more as a source of experience and information than as an overlord. I have the authority to make things go my way, but I don't use it to bludgeon people. Instead, I function as a leader and guide.

"An interesting dynamic has come out of this. Now my people really want me at those meetings. They look forward to my input, in part because I can often contribute something significant, but equally important, because I look forward to their input as well.

"The transition from micromanager to manager who gives his people significant latitude has brought two powerful forms of return:

"1. I'm a more effective manager.

"2. I'm having more fun with the process."

An interview with Dr. Kenneth Rosen:

Q. How did you manage to break your old managerial habits, and make the transition from being a micromanager to a manager who gives his people significant latitude?

A. Harvard gave me a broader view of the world than I had been used to, sitting here in Connecticut building helicopters for thirty years. I learned a lot about how to interact with people most effectively, and that led me to do a lot of thinking about how I'd been viewed by the people who worked for me. The vision I saw wasn't entirely flattering. I realized there was an opportunity to change—and that I should seize it. The coaching approach opens the door to a new way of interfacing with your organization. But this transition can be complicated. If many have been viewing you as an autocrat, and now they're seeing you take the role of coach, sometimes it's difficult for them to accept it, and thus for you to be as effective as possible in your new role. I found it took some time for people to see me in this way, and for me to develop credibility. Then my boss, the president of the company, told me he saw some enormously positive changes in me. I think what happens is you become more confident in yourself . . . more self-assured . . . more at a point in life where you're really trying to help people, as opposed to merely striving to increase your own personal success or status. And this generosity, born of maturity, makes people want to follow your lead, work harder for you, accomplish your mutual goals. It's a principle young managers, caught up in their ambitions, are often blind to: The fact is, the more you give in terms of coaching, mentoring, empathizing—the more you will achieve in terms of measurable business goals.

Q. But don't leaders have to be authority figures? Don't they have to lead?

A. Yes. I want to make it clear that you can move too far toward coaching. And when you do, you have to be able to steer back a bit. You need to find a happy medium. It's important to think about this as you encounter each situation. There are times when a team is in complete disarray, and you must step in and provide hands-on leadership, even while you're striving to be a coach. Finding that happy medium is the true sign of an inspired and effective leader.

Q. It sounds as if you've achieved a true balance now. But in the beginning, how did you keep yourself from sliding back into your old habits?

A. Shortly before AMP, I was in the hospital for a serious medical condition. I never forgot the experience—instead I used it to put things in perspective. When I saw or heard something upsetting at meetings, rather than exploding, I would say to myself, "Is this really what's important here? Or are these people in this meeting merely struggling and need some help?" Everybody has something like that in his or her life. Whether it's a personal or career setback, a health issue or another close call, you can use the mental image of that crisis to put things in perspective when you are faced with a trying situation on the job. Instead of taking precipitous action, stop, count to ten, and get back to an awareness of how you're behaving in a managerial situation, and how you should behave. The very instant when it appears on the surface that your people need an autocratic presence may be just the time that an understanding coach can galvanize the team and get them moving toward a common goal.

In Business, Even War Heroes Have to Put Away the Sword

Micromanagement won't work when teamwork is a priority. And as the Advanced Management Program emphasizes, teamwork is essential for competing in the global arena.

No one knows the power of teamwork better than AMP graduate Moshe Levy. When he took the helm of Safeguards Technologies—a leading security firm— he brought to bear an authoritarian style honed in the crucible of four Israeli wars. As a highly decorated military commander whose arm was blown off during the Yom Kippur War, Levy earned his nation's highest battlefield accolade, Hero of Israel. No doubt this decisive man, with zero patience and a take-no-prisoners mentality, made for an intimidating presence in the boardroom just as he had during battle.

"I used to address customers and employees the same way: I'm the boss. I know what is best," recalls Levy. "You do what you do the way I say you should do it. I don't tolerate questions, suggestions, or feedback.

"When I look back now, I realize that I went from being a commander in the military to a dictator in business. AMP made me realize that this was self-defeating. Yes, I was decisive, but I wasn't following the best procedures for building a business. That's because I had made two major blunders:

"1. I closed the door to the valuable input I could get from others.

"2. By functioning as a dictator, I failed to build, nurture, and leverage the power of teamwork.

"All of this came into sharp focus at AMP, and it proved to be just the kind of jolt to the system that I needed to take corrective action. Right out of the gate, I started to treat customers differently. Before AMP, I would say to customers: You know your business and I know security. So leave the security to me.

"My people presented customers with the systems we believed were right for them. If they wanted to contribute to the process we told them—sometimes diplomatically, sometimes not—we don't need or want your help. But we really did need their input. Many of our systems were plagued with problems after we installed them precisely because we excluded the customer from the design process. No longer. More than anything else, AMP taught me to listen. To collaborate. To question our customers. To share information. And to develop teams to work together on system concepts, design, and installation. Customers are much happier now because installations are running smoother and there is a tighter fit between customer wants and needs and what we deliver at the outset."

The new leadership perspectives Levy gained, fused with his real-world application of fresh approaches after the AMP experience, have culminated in a strategy we'll call:

MOSHE LEVY'S FIVE STEPS TO POWERFUL TEAM BUILDING

1. Abandon the idea that you know it all. You don't. No matter how long you've been in business, you can still learn from customers, employees, and vendors.
2. Collaborate, don't dictate. By encouraging your constituents to contribute ideas, suggestions, criticism, and feedback, you will give them the sense of teamwork that makes everyone more productive.
3. When visiting customers, listen before you sell. People want the opportunity to explain in detail what they need. And they want to know that their vendors value their input and factor it into the product or service.
4. Resist the urge to dominate company meetings. Listening to the boss issue a stream of orders isn't a meeting—it's a one-person show that violates the spirit of teamwork.
5. Give people the freedom to make mistakes. As a military commander, Levy told his troops, "Make a mistake and you're dead." But in business, you can make a mistake and have the chance to learn, regroup, and try again—all the wiser from your experience.

The Quest for Perfection Is a Sure Sign of a Small Thinker

At the start of our careers, we're all specialists: engineers, accountants, salespeople, programmers, actuaries—men and women with narrow corridors of functional expertise.

As we seek to propel our careers and rise through the ranks, we tend to apply our talent, intelligence, and energies to sharpening this focus in pursuit of a higher form of specialization. To become an engineer's engineer. An accountant's accountant. A star salesperson in a galaxy of sales stars.

It's the quest for personal best—measured by the Calvinist standard of hard work and continuous self-improvement. Although widely admired, this is not the way to get to the top of the managerial hierarchy. In fact, it is a near certain way to short-circuit one's career potential.

"The goal of specialists is to optimize individual effort," says AMP professor emeritus Hugo Uyterhoeven. "Engineers want to design the best products. Finance people want to find the most effective means of controlling overhead . . . and on and on. But to rise to the ranks of senior management, you must forgo this quest for personal perfection, seeking instead to balance the skills and capabilities of the specialists working for you. You must make the transformation from a member of a team to the planner, coach, and facilitator of team performance."

Many executives find this transformation difficult or impossible to accomplish, precisely because they cannot abandon the focus on personal perfection. To do so, they must have the realization that in today's global arena, individual perfection is not as desirable as a high level of collective performance.

"For example, the violinist is a principal member of the orchestra," Uyterhoeven continues. "The better the orchestra, the more of a virtuoso the violinist must be for the privilege of playing with his or her peers. Perfection is this musician's quest. But unlike the musician, the maestro must balance the individual musician's quest with the goal of producing a complete sound that exceeds the sum of the orchestra's parts. This requires acceptance of two concepts that are problematic for specialty-focused executives:

"1. They must shift their focus from self-indulgent perfection to organizational excellence.

"2. They must require that their individual players forgo the quest for personal best in concert with the group effort. The violin virtuoso whose performance upstages the delicate balance of the orchestra's holistic sound must be required to sacrifice ego gratification for the sake of the group. Achieving this delicate balance is a prerequisite of effective management."

It is a challenge that increases in degree of difficulty as one rises up the ladder of career success. That's due to an often hidden paradox that can blindside managers. Think of it this way: The more senior your rank in the company, the more you will be required to manage strong-willed and independent-minded people—many of whom will think they are smarter than you and who are gunning for your position. This is where the stakes and the rewards of achieving true collaboration rise exponentially. Harnessing your abilities to lead through the power of intellect, will, persistence, and vision creates synergies that propel successful companies in the quest for, and achievement of, competitive advantage.

First Find Your Comfort Zone— Then Find a Way Out

Even the most indispensable executive is often forced to leave the office for a week or more. Due to vacation, company retreat, or illness, he gives up the reins and lets the staff run the show. For many this experience is fraught with fear that something terrible will go wrong. But in most cases, the executive discovers to his surprise that everything runs smoothly in his absence. This leads to an epiphany: The people I've trained do their work so well, they don't need me to focus on the things I've been focusing on. In fact, the best thing I can do is to break with my routine and experiment and explore new approaches and broaden my vision.

For most of us, the easiest thing to do each morning is to pick up where we left off the day before. That's our comfort zone. But success in business doesn't come from being comfortable. With this in mind, the wisest course is to identify a new opportunity and pursue it:

- Explore new markets to penetrate.
- Consider the development of new products or services.

- Test the application of new technologies.
- Reengineer your organizational structure and your methods of motivating people.

The idea is to set dual strategies in motion and allow yourself the time to think and create a vision based on the emerging opportunities for your business while empowering your staff to run the business unit day to day (naturally, with oversight on your part). This intelligent and productive division of duties provides for a well-managed enterprise with strong growth potential—and assures your indispensability for the long term.

Sometimes this means going beyond your staff's capabilities as well as your own, to secure a level of expertise that is unavailable in-house.

"When I was running my company, a conspiracy was brewing beneath the surface," noted the late Wilson Harrell, founder and chief executive of Formula 409. "One of my employees—the wife of a Teamsters official—was secretly organizing the workforce. She was so good at operating beneath the radar that by the time I discovered what was going on, the employees were about to take a vote on accepting union representation.

"As a lifelong entrepreneur with little patience for unions, my knee-jerk response was to fire everyone who supported the Teamsters. And I probably would have, were it not for my experience at AMP. As part of our training, Harvard had us sit on both sides of the bargaining table—at one point as a representative of management and then as a union negotiator. This dual perspective provided valuable insights into the complexities of labor-management negotiations and made me see how incredibly difficult it can be to reach an acceptable settlement. I also learned that unless you respect the process, you'll wind up facing a complex legal problem. Needless to say, firing everyone won't cut it.

"What did I do? I asked an adviser for the name of the best labor lawyer in the country, hired him immediately, and gave him wide latitude in dealing with the union. Then I gathered my managers and told them to back off and let the pro be our one and only contact with the union. Anyone without dedicated expertise in the field would likely take an incendiary issue and put a match to it.

"Successful entrepreneurs and CEOs have key traits in common, not the least of which is the feeling that when a crisis erupts, no one is better equipped than us to put out the fire. But AMP teaches you to assess, candidly and honestly, what you can't do best as well as what you can. That's the kind of reality check you don't get when you're at the top, surrounded by sycophants, making decisions in a vacuum."

ENLIGHTENED LEADERSHIP: THE POWER OF THE PERPETUAL STUDENT

The first thing AMP participants experience is an awkward transition from the office to the classroom. During the first days of training, the students feel they are obligated to reconnect with the people and the issues that had occupied virtually all of their waking moments before arriving at the Harvard Business School campus.

But when this impulse, this feeling of missing out, passes, a new revelation about the power of learning takes its place.

"As I became immersed in the Harvard program, it struck me that a leader should be a perpetual student," says AMP graduate Roy Richards. "Returning to the classroom is the best way to expand your base of knowledge above and beyond what you are likely to learn in the course of daily business. Based on this insight, I pledged to take some form of training every year. Schooling helps to fill the gap in your skills and experience and makes you more effective as a business manager. For example, I'm now going back to school to learn Spanish. A half billion people live south of Texas—and only one third of them have electricity. Because we're in the electric power business, I need to know more about these people, the way they live, the best methods of marketing to them, and the obstacles that stand in my way. Learning Spanish will serve as my passport for getting immersed in the culture, and this is critical for achieving success on a global scale."

Even when ultimate success is achieved, inspired leaders seize every opportunity to gain more knowledge. They understand that this wisdom can be applied to any challenge they come up against. An experience of my own reinforces this thinking. On a recent vacation on the Caribbean island of Anguilla, I met a successful entrepreneur—the owner of a luxury resort and head of a global hedge fund, who had earned his fortune creating the largest discount store chain in South Africa.

When the entrepreneur was deep into building his retail operation he received an unexpected letter from Sam Walton, founder and chairman of Wal-Mart, at the time the richest man in the world. Walton's brief note to an absolute stranger contained a request. Could he visit the entrepreneur in Cape Town to learn his secrets of successful retailing? Considering that Walton's retail empire—and his personal success— dwarfed the South African's, his request to learn from a man who would qualify more as a protégé than a mentor was extraordinary. Naturally, the entrepreneur was delighted and exhilarated by Walton's interest in his business, and he promptly invited the legendary merchant to visit him in South Africa. Soon after, Walton—who made the long trip in his customary coach class seat—arrived at the entrepreneur's office ready to do business. This meant inspecting as many stores as he could cram into a busy schedule—not as a visiting dignitary, but as a student of retailing. Walton examined floor designs, checked inventories, studied computer systems, and inspected loading docks. With notebook in hand, he interviewed the fellow retailer, queried employees, questioned customers, and talked with vendors. All the while he took copious notes, keeping a detailed record of all that he learned. A record he could review on the plane ride back to his home base in Bentonville, Arkansas, and save as a reference.

Although it seems extraordinary that the most successful retailer in history would leap at the chance to learn from a merchant seemingly far too small to earn a place on his radar screen, the episode reflects a pattern that ran throughout Walton's career. In many ways, he conducted his life as a voyage of continuous learning. Wherever he traveled he used the opportunity to examine, question, inspect, study, and absorb every fact that he believed would expand his base of knowledge, widen his perspective, and, in the final analysis, make himself a better retailer—and a superior businessman.

Walton's quest for continuous learning extended beyond the realm of retail logistics. Equally important were insights on merchandising, employee motivation, customer service, advertising, public relations, and competitive strategies. He never measured the relative size of the people and companies he studied. Rather, he based his approach on the humble but brilliant insight that anyone who had achieved any level of success had something to teach him. That Sam Walton had done it all and achieved the pinnacle in his industry was considered irrelevant in the context of the Walton philosophy: He who knows the most, and continues to learn the most, wins.

Although Walton never attended AMP, his deeply ingrained curiosity and sense of wonderment about the complex dynamics of retailing reflect the program's focus on the importance of being a perpetual student. As the following section illustrates, this is especially important as you seek to build an effective organization—one that can compete today, as well as anticipate and respond to change before it occurs.

2

TUNING THE STRADIVARIUS:
Building World-Class Organizations

People selected to attend the Advanced Management Program seek to achieve change.

Whether you are a member of senior management or a junior executive on the way up, you must learn to shape your department, unit, division, or company to respond to changing dynamics in order to achieve your business plan objectives. This is a daunting challenge.

When seeking to change an organization of any size, managers run head-on into Newton's Law that a body at rest tends to stay at rest. Advocates for change are greeted with suspicion, anger, resistance, and, in more cases than anyone wants to admit, even sabotage. AMP teaches you how to bring about effective change in this crocodile swamp of egos, jealousy, and power plays.

Although we live in a culture that worships and rewards great business leaders, anyone who makes the mistake of thinking that the cult of personality is more important than the organization he or she creates is not only wrong, but destined to fail. General Electric's CEO Jack Welch is not a legend because he is a superb manager on a personal level, but because he has created an extraordinary organization that succeeds in dozens of diverse businesses, vanquishes competitors, and is continually at the vanguard of change. Welch's greatness lies in his ability to achieve two complex goals simultaneously:

1. Selecting superior managers to run GE's operating units. For the most part, these are entrepreneurial men and women dedicated to eliminating bureaucracy and building businesses.
2. Creating a financial reporting structure that enables Welch to monitor the managers' individual performance by the numbers. More than memos, surveys, or subjective analyses, these statistics tell Welch how well, or how poorly, his field marshals are performing.

Under Welch's watch, managers have wide latitude in building their GE units, as long as the numbers demonstrate the wisdom of their ways. When they don't, Welch has the data to act quickly. Because of the organization Welch has built, senior executives run far-flung businesses in entrepreneurial fashion. It is a model of exceptional performance everyone can learn from.

This section helps you explore your organizational options for change. It focuses on innovations both simple and complex that can assist you in building a stronger, more competitive organization.

LEVERAGING THE CHANGE EQUATION: $D \times M \times P > \text{COST}$

It's a familiar refrain among corporate managers:

I can't do what I need to do because the culture won't let me do it. This company resists change, fights it at every turn, and stops initiative dead in its tracks.

More often than not, there is truth to this. Institutional bias, coupled with the "not invented here" syndrome, keeps many sound ideas from gaining the objective assessment they deserve. Fortunately, there is an effective means of overcoming this resistance. It is based around a relatively simple approach: Separate the human issues from the business issues.

A closer look reveals that when you complain your company's culture is blocking you, you are really complaining that people are blocking you by putting up hurdles and obstacles that serve their personal interests. All too often, you put up with this for fear of igniting a feud and, in the process, being branded a troublemaker.

In this situation you are permitting business goals to be subjugated to your adversaries' personal goals. This prohibits you from accomplishing your mission and leaves you with only one acceptable course of action. You must challenge the culture and dare to make enemies among your peers when this is what it takes to achieve identified corporate objectives.

The first step should be to assemble a cross-functional team of like-minded colleagues to scale the cultural barriers and create change. Look for kindred spirits in engineering, marketing, and manufacturing.

The broader based your coalition, the more likely you'll be able to penetrate the layers of resistance and make significant progress.

AMP considers this to be a central component of your managerial duty.

"We all know the common refrain 'I don't want to rock the boat,'" says Professor Michael Beer. "Well, I say nonsense to that. I charge managers with responsibility for rocking the boat. Your job is to promote the dialogue that creates change. Even if your scope of responsibility is small, you can create ripples that generate change throughout the organization. I've developed a formula for leading change:

$$\text{Change} = D \times M \times P > \text{Cost}$$

"This holds that three factors—Dissatisfaction, Business Organizational Model, and Process—are critical to achieving change and that D, M, and P must overcome, or be greater than, the cost of change (which is the loss felt by the people in the organization when change occurs). This should not be thought of as a cost-benefit equation. Instead, it is a driving force versus barrier equation. The cost is the barrier, and if the costs are high, then you have to sharpen the level of the dissatisfaction, create a better business model, and craft your process ever more carefully to overcome the cost."

Let's take a closer look at Beer's change equation:

$$D = \text{Dissatisfaction}$$

"To function as a leader, you must create dissatisfaction with the status quo. Because change is inevitable, you are better off leading it than reacting to it."

M = Business Organizational Model

"Change for the sake of change never did anyone any good. That's why you need a business model that provides strategic direction for the change you create. Your model must answer the question: What kind of organization do we need to achieve success now and in the future?

"The model must be specific, addressing the kinds of people, policies, strategies, assets, structure, and shared values that are critical to achieving the mission."

P = Process

"People often think that to achieve change, they need one or more tangible assets: technology, talented personnel, or national advertising. This may be true, but to bring it all together they need a process. In the final analysis, process facilitates change and helps direct it toward targeted goals.

"Returning to my key point, remember that Dissatisfaction x Model x Process must be greater than the cost of change, with cost measured in terms of loss—loss of job security, loss of compensation, or loss of personal status," Beer says. "Unless the forces for change are powerful enough to overcome the loss that people feel as a result of this change, the change will not occur.

"A case in point occurred at Apple Computer in the 1980s. At the time John Sculley came in as Apple's

CEO, the culture was heavily vested in the company's founding concept of innovative technology making a difference in the world. This concept formed Apple's identity—and its people were proud of it. When Sculley sought to create change at Apple, the sense of loss was enormous. The R&D people, who were long the power at Apple, felt the greatest loss, the greatest threat, and for this reason they precluded Sculley from reframing the company's strategy and organization.

"In essence, Sculley failed to create sufficient dissatisfaction with the status quo. He did a poor job of articulating his strategy for the company, and for related organizational change that would give people reason to buy in. He failed to fully think through how to get the driving forces of change to overcome the barriers to change."

This case study prompts an important question:

How can a manager make the driving forces of change greater than the resistance to change?

"Start by raising dissatisfaction," Beer says. "How do you do that? You engage people by getting them out to talk to customers, and you get employees to tell you what's wrong with your company. This begins to uncover many of the faults lying beneath the surface. People rarely see that things aren't as good as they appear day to day—that there is risk in clinging to the status quo. Once motivation has been developed, which is essentially what dissatisfaction is about, you've got to move on to create a better business model. Get your top team and other key people together to begin to have a discussion on how you want to reorganize, restructure, and change the pattern of behavior to be able to respond to the problems you've surfaced. Then institute a process of high involvement for accomplishing your solution."

BOTTOM-UP LEARNING: HOW EMPLOYEE CRITICISM CAN MAKE YOU A BETTER MANAGER

Managers are often the biggest barriers to change. Confident that they are smart and in control, they see little reason to change. If employees have a different view (as is often the case), this view is rarely expressed publicly. That's because no one wants to tell the manager that her strategy or approach to managing is damaging the company's current or long-term goals.

This is precisely why managers must demand candid and continuous feedback from their constituents. You can achieve this result by subjecting yourself to the 360 degree process: Empower employees, vendors, and peers to rate your management performance. Promise anonymity, and candid opinions will come from every direction. This may make you feel uncomfortable and vulnerable, but that may be just what you need to identify deficiencies and recognize the need to make changes and take action.

"For a manager, acceptance of the status quo is deadly," says the chief information systems officer for a global manufacturer of transportation equipment and AMP graduate. "AMP drives it into your head that you have to be relentless in fighting against it. I put this approach into action immediately after my AMP experience.

"There I was urging that we invest in technology to meet an evolving global standard that was posing a serious threat to our product architecture. And there's the CFO, representing the company's long-established cultural posture that we'll worry about it when the time comes. Well, the time had come, and if we waited another year to act, the Germans would steal a significant percentage of our market share.

"When my team decided to act, I took the lead, because I knew it was imperative for my department and my company. In doing so, I abandoned any concern about causing confrontation and focused instead on the overwhelming business issues at stake. There's a critical lesson here: Once you put mission over politics, you can break down the most daunting roadblocks."

PLACE YOURSELF IN A FISHBOWL: EMERGE A BETTER LEADER WITH THE ORGANIZATIONAL FITNESS PROFILE

Even the best leaders can be blind to the core issues, obstacles, and barriers that prevent their business units from achieving optimal performance. This is often because personal and organizational weaknesses are hidden within the business structure. By shielding the culprits, including senior management, from blame and accountability there is a risk that the business unit will put forth a second-rate performance. Professor Michael Beer and consultant Russell A. Eisenstat have developed an innovative process, the Organizational Fitness Profile (OFP), that can help X-ray your organization, identify the soft spots, and take corrective action.

The OFP process starts with the leader and senior managers committing themselves to an inquiry that will delve into the efficiency of their organization and leadership principles. Next, they set ground rules for nondefensive communication. Then they define their game plan and objectives and commission a task force of their best people to interview customers and employees. They all ask the basic question: What do you perceive as the strengths and/or barriers of this company or business unit as we seek to implement our strategy and accomplish our goals?

The feedback gained from these interviews is completed and analyzed by the task force during a three-day Organizational Fitness Profile meeting. The first day of that meeting is the most emotionally charged because the task force usually has bad news to report. As such, those in attendance are often quite anxious. Some participants will even wear buttons reading "Don't Shoot the Messenger."

As the process moves on to the fishbowl, nondefensive communication comes into play. The task force sits around a table in the middle of a room, surrounded by a U-shaped conference table where senior management sits. The task force begins by reporting what it has found in its interviews, using a set of prearranged topics as its anchor. These topics relate to a classic model of how to analyze an organization. For example, one of the typical themes is whether customers and employees perceive the top team as ineffective.

Other topics the task force reports on include:

1. A top-down or laissez-faire style of leadership on the part of management that is either too directive or too hands-off.
2. How management fails to engage the organization effectively.
3. Poor teamwork and coordination across various functions in the company.
4. An unclear strategy or many conflicting priorities concerning what's going on in various parts of the organization.
5. Poor vertical communication: People don't know what the people at the top are thinking.
6. A relative lack of leadership/managerial skills in the organization.

Once the task force's report is complete, the top team of managers wrestles with whatever conclusions are drawn, including how well they are leading the organization; how they can change their behavior; and how to restructure the organization so as to enable it to transform itself.

An interview with Professor Michael Beer on the Organizational Fitness Profile:

Q. How do you get task force members to be candid in their findings when the bad news they may have to report impacts their superiors, peers, and friends?

A. The mechanism of the fishbowl is self-protective in

the sense that the task force is not talking about their own opinions. They are talking about data obtained from others, and they are presenting their findings as a group—not as individuals. In my experience, there has never been a failure of getting the feedback on the table. The failures are in management not following up and effectively addressing the fault lines that the research reveals. But even the least-motivated managers are hard-pressed to ignore the messengers completely. That's because they have asked their best people to participate in the task force. So the managers are caught in a bind: They either reject what their best people say or pay attention to it. We have found that most top management understand that what they're hearing is in fact the unvarnished truth. They may not like it, it may be difficult to deal with, but it's the truth and they've got to deal with it.

Q. What do you mean when you say that the top management team and the task force have to commit to the ground rules of nondefensive communication?

A. The premise is that we're here to talk about some very difficult issues, and we have to be open, candid, and flexible. Most important, we have to depersonalize the questions and responses. For example, if you are on the receiving end of feedback, you need to have a nondefensive response. You don't say, Where'd you get that information? You can't blame others for the data. You've got to ask questions and try to be open to exploring the issues. And if you're on the reporting side, you have to provide quotes and examples of the feedback you received from the interviews. Again, the key point is that the task force is not talking about its own opinions. So on the receiving end, managers are told they've got to listen and ask questions for clarification and understanding; they've got to understand that perception is fact. When the organization collectively perceives something, that makes it a fact as far as the organization is concerned. And you have to deal with it.

Q. How does OFP relate to your D x M x P > Cost equation?

A. Well, a part of the OFP process uses the feedback and/or data from interviews to create dissatisfaction with the status quo within the top team. One of my findings is that most dissatisfaction, when it exists, is generally limited to the lower and middle levels of the organization. The top is insulated from it until the exposure they gain at the OFP fishbowl. That's the key outcome of the meeting. The rest of the meeting is designed to develop an improved business model—which addresses how to organize and manage differently to make business better.

Your Organizational Fitness Profile Road Map

If you think that the OFP process would be useful for your company or business unit, use the following road map for conducting the process:

1. *Orientation and Planning:* A one-day meeting led by a consultant or facilitator proceeds through the following:

First, the top management team develops a "Statement of Strategic and Organizational Direction" that articulates the links between the company's competitive context, performance goals, business strategy, and needed organizational and cultural changes. This statement is used both to communicate and explain the logic behind the strategy and as a stimulus to collect organizational information on barriers to implementation.

After the statement is issued, a task force composed of a cross section of middle managers from different functions or businesses one or two levels below the top team is appointed to collect the organizational information.

2. *Data Collection:* Members of the employee task force are trained to conduct open-ended interviews inside and outside the organization about specific management practices and arrangements that help or hinder the implementation of specific strategies. Consultants also conduct interviews with members of the top management team about their effectiveness.

3. *Meeting:* An OFP meeting is held wherein the task force feeds back the data it has collected. This is followed by an analysis of the organization's effectiveness. A plan is then established to implement this

new organizational vision. The OFP meeting is structured as follows:

Step 1: Seated in an outer circle, the top management team listens to the task force (seated in an inner circle) discuss its findings. This fishbowl process is carefully orchestrated to allow the task force to present an accurate and complete picture of even the most politically sensitive barriers to strategy implementation. Guided by ground rules for nondefensive communication, the top team dialogues with the employee task force at the end of each presentation.

The task force departs after the fishbowl concludes. The consultants then feed back a summary of the major themes from their interviews with the members of the top management team. If the interviews suggest that the role or style of any team member, including the general manager, is helping or impeding top team effectiveness, these issues are discussed.

Step 2: The top management team uses a systemic model to assess the consequences of organizational deficiencies identified by the task force and then evaluates their causes.

Step 3: Using the Organizational Fitness Profile, the top management team develops a broad model and vision of how the company should be redesigned to implement the new strategy more effectively. An implementation plan is also developed.

Focus is placed on projects that directly improve business performance as well as on contextual issues. The latter include the organization's design and the top team's functioning—particularly roles, responsibilities, meetings, and decision making. Projects are typically conducted by consultant-assisted cross-functional teams, and are reviewed by the senior management group.

Step 4: Following the OFP meeting, the top management team gathers with the task force to review what they have heard and what they plan to do. Meeting separately, the task force evaluates the proposed changes and gives its reaction to management. This serves as a useful reality check on the adequacy of senior management's plans. This step establishes a partnership between top management and employees in managing change.

Step 5: In those cases where OFP is most effective, it serves as a template for ongoing organizational learning and improvement. This includes:

- A continuing role for the employee task force in evaluating organizational progress and identifying areas of opportunity.
- Implementing a project management system for the ongoing commissioning, conduct, and review of organizational improvement efforts.
- The periodic readministration (approximately every one to two years) of the Or-

ganizational Fitness Profile for the business as a whole.

Evolution + Revolution = Solution

How you change a business unit to adapt to shifting markets is a matter of management style. For most managers, evolutionary change is the mode of choice. Under this approach, corporate leaders set direction, allocate responsibilities, and establish reasonable timelines for making changes and achieving objectives.

This evolutionary change is relatively tranquil, diplomatic, and painless. But its fatal flaw is that it's rarely fast enough or comprehensive enough to move ahead of the curve in an evolving world.

In situations when timing is crucial to success, revolutionary change is demanded. When the stakes are high, and the response time is short, abrupt and sometimes disruptive change may be required to keep the company competitive.

"AMP made me recognize that dramatic downsizing and reengineering—like the widespread streamlining that swept through American industry in the early 1990s—can be imperative, especially when viewed in the context of escalating global competition," says a former AMP graduate who is now a vice president at a global aircraft company. "When faced with market-driven urgency there is precious little time to plod along, tinkering with the organization on an incremental basis. To be truly competitive in times like this, companies must get more efficient and productive rapidly. Instead of waiting for attrition and other characteristics of evolutionary change to take hold, managers faced with the urgent need to respond must consider revolutionary change that calls for eliminating people, plants, products, procedures—swiftly and decisively. This approach can also swing too far to one extreme by creating an organizational culture that is so impatient, and so focused on change, that it fails to give new initiatives and new personnel time to take root, stabilize, and grow. What's more, it creates a high-tension environment that intimidates rather than nurtures people, leaving them with little or no emotional investment in the company. In this context, the leader has failed to pursue a balanced and pragmatic approach that responds as needed to real-world conditions as opposed to internal political biases."

The idea is to preside over a mix of evolutionary change and revolutionary action. Thus, for the leader, the critically important equation is: Evolution + Revolution = Appropriate Business Solution.

Desmond Bonnar, AMP graduate, managing director (Scotland/Ireland) of Thames Water PLC and formerly CEO of Scotland's Lothian and Edinburgh Enterprise, Ltd., believes this kind of leadership is related, in great measure, to the ability to identify and exploit what he calls connectivity.

"Management is all about the process of change," Bonnar says. "How to stay ahead of it, master it, benefit from the opportunities it brings. There is no map for doing this, no published set of rules. But there is a methodology. I like to equate the process to the way the human body functions. The central nervous system is composed of millions of connections that provide the brain with a wealth of options for responding to every physical and intellectual stimulant. This allows human beings to move with agility, grace, and speed rather than like lumbering robots.

"Companies have similar connectivity in the form of the minds and talents of the people that make up the organization. But these resources are often underutilized. That's the case when all of the strategy and all of the know-how about dealing with customers and building the business is considered to be the exclusive preserve of senior management. When this happens, the company's connectivity between management and the people at the front line is seriously diminished, limiting the range of offensive and defensive options the business can take when confronted with problems and opportunities. This confines the company's movements to highly structured, established ways of working, depriving it of the subtlety, agility, and nuance that is so critical for responding effectively to change.

"Leaders with savvy recognize that they can leverage connectivity by tapping into the pool of knowledge that rests with front-line employees. These people have the most current and accurate perspective on customers—what they really think, how and what they buy, and when and why they switch to a competitor's product or services.

"For example, IBM's turnaround under Lou Gerstner can be credited in part to their doing a better job of learning from the bottom up. They knew how to encourage and utilize connectivity. We did this at Lothian and Edinburgh Enterprise, Ltd., by going directly to our employees and asking them to:

- recommend what our strategic priorities should be;
- advise us on our investment priorities for the next five years; and
- suggest the changes we should make in the business.

"As managers, our obligation is to listen and act, putting the knowledge resource of our employees to work by enhancing connectivity. In this way we can expand options and remain ahead of the learning curve that is the inevitable by-product of change."

LEADERSHIP 101: THE JACK WELCH WAY

If there is a true believer in the importance of effecting organizational change, it is General Electric's CEO Jack Welch. Although he is the celebrated leader of a global manufacturer often noted for its technological prowess, Welch has utilized a very human process to drive change through GE's vast organization.

Some years ago, Welch found himself coming to grips with a problem that had been floating in and out of his peripheral vision for months. In locations throughout GE, local managers were operating with Chinese walls separating managerial functions and the rank and file. In this insulated environment, employee questions, gripes, and feedback were discouraged. All too often, GE employees were expected to keep their hands busy and their mouths shut.

Welch viewed this as anathema. He believed in creating an open, collaborative workplace where everyone's opinion was welcome. Determined to harness the collective power of GE employees, Welch developed Work-Out: a series of town hall meetings conducted by GE management (Welch included), and designed to accomplish four key goals:

- Encourage employees to share their views in a collaborative culture.
- Vest greater responsibility, power, and accountability with front-line employees.
- Eliminate wasteful, irrational, and repetitive steps in the work process (which would come to light through employee feedback).
- Dismantle the boundaries that prevented the cross-pollination of ideas and efforts. In the Welch-led GE culture, traditional barriers dividing employees, co-workers, and management would give way to tethers of interdisciplinary and interdepartmental cooperation.

From Welch's perspective, Work-Out—and the free flow of ideas it creates—is all about redefining relationships between boss and subordinates (Quinn 1994).

"The individual is the fountainhead of creativity and innovation, and we are struggling to get all of our people to accept the countercultural truth that often the best way to manage people is just to get out of their way. Only by releasing the energy and fire of our employees can we achieve the decisive, continuous productivity advantages that will give us the freedom to compete and win in any business anywhere on the globe."

As Welch wrote in a letter to shareholders:

"My view of the 1990s is based on the liberation of the workplace. If you want to get the benefit of everything employees have, you've got to free them—make everybody a participant. Everybody has to know everything, so they can make the right decisions by themselves.

"In the old culture, managers got their power from secret knowledge: profit margins, market share, and all that. But once you share that information with everyone, it often turns out that the emperor has no clothes. In the new culture, the role of the leader is to express a vision, get buy-in, and implement it. That calls for open, caring relations with every employee, and face-to-face communication. People who can't convincingly articulate a vision won't be successful. But those who can will become even more open—because success breeds self-confidence."

Six Rules for Successful Leadership from GE's Jack Welch

- Control your destiny, or someone else will.
- Face reality as it is, not as it was or as you wish it were.
- Be candid with everyone.
- Don't manage, lead.
- Change before you have to.
- If you don't have a competitive advantage, don't compete.

"Often, when people study Welch, they believe his philosophy holds that if a business unit isn't the market leader in its industry, management has failed," says AMP graduate Bill Griffin, president of K&W Manufacturing. "But I have a different take on Welch's case. I believe his approach can apply to small companies like the one I'm running now. We may never rise to the position of market leader: We're starting from too small a base to achieve that. But we can aspire to achieve a more important feat—to become number one performers in our industry. If your business produces the best product or service at the best price and terms, customers will come to you regardless of your position or the industry size rankings.

"View it this way: Our company used to be much larger. Sloppy performance throughout the manufacturing and distribution process caused us to shrink. Now, people still say, 'Oh, you're with X, we used to buy from you.' Now we've improved our performance dramatically and customers are buying from us once again. In the year since we've vowed to be number one, we've doubled in business volume—and are on target for a threefold increase."

Jack Welch's respect for the individual as a pivotal force in organizational change at GE reflects a continuum of successful business management that was brought to light by another astute corporate leader and observer, James F. Lincoln, a member of the founding family of Lincoln Electric Company. For more than a century, Lincoln Electric has been one of the nation's most respected manufacturers. The company's performance and durability are attributable, in great measure, to a distinct organizational philosophy. Lincoln Electric has always placed a high value on an open, collaborative organization that respects its employees and treats them as integral members of a team. James Lincoln's case study, Observations on Management, can serve as a blueprint for today's managers seeking to motivate people, achieve exceptional results, and emulate Lincoln Electric's performance.

James F. Lincoln's Observations on Management

- Many incentives are far more effective than money. Status is a much greater incentive.
- The worker is not a man apart. He has the same needs, aspirations, and reactions as the industrialist. A worker will not cooperate on any program that will penalize him.
- The industrial manager is very conscious of his company's need of uninterrupted income. He is completely oblivious, though, to the worker's same need.
- Most companies are run by hired managers, under the control of stockholders. As a result, the goal of the company has shifted from service to the customer to making the larger dividends for stockholders.
- The manager is dealing with expert workers. While you can boss these experts around in the usual lofty way, their eager cooperation will not be won.
- If a manager received the same treatment in matters of income, security, advancement, and dignity as the hourly worker, he would understand the real problem of management.

- The incentives that are most potent when properly offered are:
  Money in proportion to production.
  Status as a reward for achievement.
  Publicity of the worker's contributions and skill.
- If each person is properly rated and paid, there will not only be a fair reward to each worker but friendly and exciting competition.
- There are many forms and degrees of cooperation between the worker and the management. The worker's attitude can vary all the way from passivity to highly imaginative contributions to efficiency and progress (Berg 1973, 1983).

Consider Lincoln's last point. Then see how it resonates with recent AMP graduate and Pacific Corp. executive Mike Pittman's managerial experience.

"AMP introduced me to a concept I'll call the power of the quiet person," says Pittman. "Here's what I mean by this. Most of us are conditioned to pay a lopsided amount of attention to people with commanding personalities. The ones on your staff who jump up at a meeting and start to bring forth ideas, write them down on a board, and monopolize the conversation—they generally have the most influence on your decision-making process.

"But AMP makes you see that this person has a powerful style but that that doesn't necessarily equate to a superior mind or exceptional creativity. In fact, the quiet person—the one who isn't built with the personality to hold court at a meeting—may be the one with the most compelling ideas. You may have to seek these people out.

"One of the members of my AMP living group, a

Malaysian executive, was incredibly low-key. Judging him at first by my American standards, I thought he would have little to add to the group's thought process. But slowly and gradually as his voice emerged, we all realized he was among the smartest, most effective members of the group.

"This experience made me see, in sharp relief, how we are often quick to favor a certain style of person to the detriment of others. And when we do, we wind up hiring a group of people who tend to think and act alike. That's unacceptable. To face today's complex challenges, we need to incorporate a wide range of styles, skill sets, and perspectives. That's why it's important to encourage and bring out the power of the quiet person. This is especially true in dealing with global issues."

THREE-POINT SYSTEM FOR LINKING STRATEGY TO ACTION

Bruce Elliot, president of Labatt Breweries, Atlantic Division, has applied a grassroots management methodology—which is at the core of many AMP case studies—to unleash the power of his organization and, in the process, reshape it into a more vital and competitive enterprise.

Since assuming the presidency of Labatt's Atlantic Division in 1995, Elliot has presided over significant growth in market share, productivity, and profits. This managerial hat trick has been accomplished by creating a seamless link between strategy, employees, and management.

"After assuming the presidency of my division soon after AMP, I assessed my senior team, and found that significant changes were required. I talked to people throughout the corporation, and discovered that a number of top people in the company may have been brilliant in some ways, but lacked leadership capabilities. Some of these people had been with the company for a long time, and I guess I am from the school of thought that sees changing the head coach as a good thing. You know what the world is going to look like for your business—you're in the best position to assess people at the top and judge if they'll be able to measure up. Some people were operating in a world of status quo, or were willing to make incremental change, but I was looking for dramatic change. I would observe these managers and listen to the people that worked for them, and I would see that this kind of change was not on their list. That made what I had to do kind of easy. It was time for change. I was focused on the art of the possible—of achieving significant growth—and I couldn't let anything fool with that. This led me to replace 80 percent of my top executives, a shake-up that has proven to be a driving force for growing our business."

Elliot's use of the word "focus" is important. The ability to avoid detours by staying laser-focused on the methods that will drive the business unit toward its stated objectives is a daunting challenge. One that AMP commandos find they can address more effectively with simple, but clever, organizational devices everyone can imitate.

The following is Bruce Elliot's system for success:

- "Before you tinker with change in the bottom or the middle of an organization, start at the top. You can't make significant forward progress with a flawed management team.

- "The best companies align all of their people—from the forklift operator to executive management—against an endgame. During my first ninety days on the job, I spoke to representatives of all our employee groups, seeking their views on critical issues such as the direction we should be headed, and the changes we had to make and the resources we had to acquire, to get on track. Out of these discussions came pages of notes that led to the development of my business unit's strategic plan.

- "Build a diverse leadership group representing all of the company's key constituencies. For years, the Atlantic Division's brewery was governed by a management committee composed exclusively of company executives. We changed this governing structure to a leadership committee composed of union and management representatives who would share responsibility for plan management. We allowed for a transition period during which both groups got used to working together in a collaborative framework. We're still in the early stages, but so far the process has been highly effective and has generated an unprecedented level of mutual respect and teamwork. For the first time, we now share detailed information about the company—business plans, P&L statements, and financial projections. The thinking is that people have to understand where we are and where we are going in order to contribute effectively to our mission.

"Concerning all this, I am proud to say that we've changed people's attitudes, and that's the most important thing," says Elliot. "This engagement of the entire workforce got people involved in making decisions as part of the process. We used to have a mentality that said 'Check your brains at the door.' Now, we run the company totally differently. We get people to care about the company and the company's future—because the company's future and the employees' futures are linked. We've changed people's attitudes from 'I don't give a damn' to 'I care a lot.' "

"For years, our company spent millions of dollars on plant and equipment to boost productivity in the breweries—sometimes with only marginal results," Elliot goes on to say. "But by recognizing the importance of the hourly worker and reconfiguring the organization to give these people genuine participation in achieving our goals, we have achieved significant increases in productivity without corresponding increases in capital investments."

DRAW A STRAIGHT LINE FROM WHERE YOU ARE TO WHERE YOU WANT TO BE

"The power of focus is one of the first lessons you learn at AMP—and one of the most important," says Richard Crater, executive vice president, Massachusetts General Hospital, and AMP graduate. "Building it into your management regimen helps you stay within the framework of your key goals and keeps you pointed inexorably toward the endgame you had in mind when you launched the process. This helps to keep you from drifting, dissipating resources, and sapping the energy of your organization.

"I have found an effective way to achieve this discipline. Every time I have to make a decision, I tell myself: If I can't see a realistic link between a proposed action or expenditure and my key business goals, I'll refuse to launch an initiative or spend money. I think of it as drawing a straight line between two points—from where my business is now and where I want to take it. Everything that fails to support this is rejected as a time- and resource-wasting detour."

This simple but powerful process can be used to achieve focus quickly and effectively. For instance, a business executive is confronted with a combination of requests for travel, attendance at meetings, and funding for proposed strategies. Instinctively, he knows that the bulk of these requests will chew up time and dollars—without generating a significant return on investment. Instead of simply attending all the meetings and approving other requests in a knee-jerk or haphazard way, he applies the straight line test to each action (does the proposed action link directly to business goals?). When the answer is no or not clear, he rejects the requests, boiling down his agenda to action items that meet the new acid test.

MAKE LISTS TO TARGET
ORGANIZATIONAL GOALS

AMP graduate Bill Griffin, president of K&W Manufacturing, uses another decidedly low-tech, but powerful,
organizational device to keep his company on target.

"As a business executive, you think that you tend
to have a handle on all your major issues in the course
of your work, but when you step back and take an
objective look at it, you see that a lot is flying up at
you," says Griffin. "Invariably, some of the stuff you
need to address gets missed. You don't check it. You
don't manage it. You don't fix it if it's broken or leverage it if it's good.

"When I attended AMP, I was running a $200
million a year company. Now I'm in command of a
$1 million a year business and in this environment I
can see more clearly than ever how things fly by and
how important it is to create a personal organizational
tool or process to make sure I tend to all the significant issues, and stay on target with the company's
goals.

"I do this through a series of lists:

- "Each day, I write down what I want to achieve
  concerning my overriding business goal.
- "Each night before I leave the office, I take a few
  minutes to reflect on the day, check my list, and see
  what I accomplished and what fell by the wayside.
- "Then, I create a new list for the next day—in most
  cases, placing at the top those tasks that I failed
  to accomplish in the previous day.

"Given that my primary goal—to triple sales in a year—is always written across the top of the page, I'm always staying focused and on target. On any given day, I'll come into work determined to tackle the list in order of priorities. Of course, if a supervisor tells me I have to help put out a fire with a big customer—so much for the day's plans. If I ever get back to the list that day, there's no time to accomplish most of the tasks I set out to achieve. But adhering to the list process of personal organization minimizes the negative impact. Because I will take stock at the end of the day and create a new list based on what I have done and what still needs to be accomplished, I'm back on course the next morning.

"The power of the list extends beyond the efficient conduct of daily responsibilities. It also keeps you aligned with the macro objective—in my case, tripling sales in a year. Every company has a strategic plan. They write it up, put it in a folder, and forget about it. If you doubt that, just take a look at their plans. You'll see that once you get to page three or so, there's little connection between what the company said it would do and what it really does. That's true, in large part, because managers often manage day by day, losing view of their goals. The list process drives you to incorporate your company's goals into your daily work, helping you to stay efficient and on strategy."

An interview with Bill Griffin, president of K&W Manufacturing and an AMP graduate:

Q. How do you motivate your people to follow through on your strategic focus?
A. We use bonuses as a prime motivator.

Q. Are annual bonuses really enough to help motivate people? Doesn't that become perceived as a constant that gets paid regardless of performance?

A. We don't pay bonuses annually. We pay them monthly. This creates a tighter link between performance and reward. If you don't perform to the required level in any given month, you don't get the bonus. Period. That sends a clear message.

Q. Bonuses get many people to work harder, but how do you know their efforts are aligned with the company's strategy and that what they are doing pays off for the business?

A. Our bonuses are linked to specific performance criteria. For example, we'll say that bonuses will be paid only if production increases x percent during the course of a month. Or if orders are shipped x percent faster, and so on. This creates a direct line between employee performance, the achievement of corporate strategy, and the payment of incentives. When everyone is thinking and acting for the collective benefit, an interesting dynamic takes over: You start to see things that were camouflaged before. We had terrible production problems before we created our new system, but no one seemed to know why. Then we discovered that the equipment maintenance people came to work one hour after the production staff, so everyone would sit around idly waiting for the maintenance people to get the machines up and running. One simple change—having the maintenance people arrive before the production staff— had a big impact on performance.

Q. Does money alone prompt individuals to work

harder and identify better ways of conducting the company's business?

A. No. People want to feel appreciated. We go out of our way to make them recognize that they are appreciated a great deal. Sometimes, when we achieve something good, I'll mark the achievement with something like a catered lunch to celebrate our success. This kind of event, combined with everything else we do, creates a sense of pride around here, and has a powerful impact on people's work. Case in point: Before we changed the way we motivate people here, orders used to be shipped in six to eight weeks. Now, orders go out the door the next day—or at least within the week.

Q. What do you do when people fail to respond to your incentives, financial or otherwise—when they simply work at inferior levels, no matter what you do to try to change that?

A. We discuss the problem with the individual. Our policy is really quite straightforward: People who fail to perform are warned. We offer them additional training and, in some cases, the opportunity to move to a different position within the company. If their performance remains poor, we let them go. In some companies a culture of leniency tolerates mediocre performance on the job. Managers fail to fire people, preferring to adopt a policy of tolerance. At our company managers recognize that the department's measurable performance will be jeopardized by mediocrity, putting their own jobs and bonuses at risk. So if people don't perform, the managers make a change.

MOTIVATE SUBORDINATES TO EMBRACE CHANGE

Peformance-incentive levers can be powerful forces for change. They are especially useful in driving those who have lacked direction or initiative. But what about those who view change as a threat and set out to halt it? For these individuals keeping the company just where it is protects their jobs, their salaries, their status and lifestyles—or so they believe. In many cases, they create formidable roadblocks that stall progress.

This presents a difficult challenge for the change-minded manager. On one hand she wants to keep her company at the vanguard. On the other she wants to be fair and reasonable in dealing with employees.

It's the "fair and reasonable" side of the argument that can trip you up. Sure, you must give those employees who are slow to embrace change another opportunity to do so. You can either give them a pep talk or move them into another job. But AMP teaches you the hard fact that in most cases you still have to be more aggressive.

Take moving an employee from a position where they are not performing well—measured by their inability or unwillingness to respond to change—to a job where it is assumed they will raise their level of performance. It usually doesn't work. People who subperform at one job do the same wherever you place them. Whereas those who are committed to superior performance rarely deliver anything else, no matter what the assignment.

"When we are identifying employees who appear to

be mired in the status quo, we ask them cordially, 'Are you willing to change?'" says Miles Greer, of Savannah Electric (AMP Class of 1996). "We're specific about what that means and what we want them to do. Those who respond positively are given the opportunity to get on the same page with us. If their intentions are good, but they lack the skills or experience to measure up, we'll offer help in the form of training, mentoring, etc. However, if they fail to respond, we tell them they are better off looking for work elsewhere.

"The refusal to accept mediocre performance goes against our industry's tradition of shifting resources to accommodate poor performers, but we can no longer compete based on this traditional approach. Anyone who thinks that it's harmless to make exceptions for a few people is missing an important point. It's not a few people who are at stake, it's the corporate culture. By permitting those who resist or retaliate against change to remain in the company, you broadcast a message that suggests supporting the company's mission statement is optional. Even worse, you permit the least-committed employees to taint and influence the attitude and performance of their peers. When that happens, the culture loses its edge and the company pays a steep price.

"For example, at Savannah Electric we recognized we had to make big changes in marketing and customer service to compete in a changing world. We achieved that by making adjustments in our organizational structure. Sometimes, these changes are counterintuitive, such as reassigning our power distribution engineer from the engineering department to the marketing department. I took this step because service outages can have a huge impact on business customers. Without power for lights, computers, production equipment, fax machines, etc., companies can be stopped in their tracks. Naturally, the faster we put them back on line, the better they feel about us, but we wanted to do more than fix a technical snafu. We wanted to demonstrate concern and sensitivity to our customers' predicament so that we could gain some points with them. That's why I placed those people responsible for restoring power in the marketing department, teaming them with peers whose job it is to make customers happy and to sell our services. This has changed our engineers' perspective on outages from a technical issue to a customer service mission. This change of focus has contributed significantly to our 35 percent increase in customer satisfaction scores since the restructuring was initiated."

Savannah Electric has taken these critical steps to promote change and raise the bar on customer service:

- Compensation for every employee who comes in contact with customers—from engineers to meter readers—is based, in part, on their service ratings.
- Senior management meets with each functional group to explain and promote the company's service ethic and to encourage employee feedback on where the company is dropping the ball and how it can take corrective action.
- Management follows up on sound employee suggestions and rewards employees for their contributions.

What Savannah Electric has discovered is that once you open the gates and encourage employees to serve as agents of change, you must demonstrate that their input will have a real-world impact on the way your company does business.

AMP helps managers discover the most effective means for achieving significant change. Breakthrough change. A change that identifies the realities of the business environment and reorders them so that a new force is able to leverage, rather than resist, those realities in order to achieve a competitive advantage.

AMP demonstrates that without this critical puzzle piece in place, companies, departments, and business units of all sizes are left with mission statements that, no matter how eloquent, are really toothless anthems that may fire the spirit but leave no means of achieving an end.

The program recognizes this and makes the critical transition from the conceptual to the pragmatic. The Advanced Management Program powerfully drives home the point that ideas and action are inexorably linked in the best-run companies—creating a seamless bridge from thought to insight to action.

3

THE MIND IS MIGHTIER THAN THE SWORD: Competitive Strategies and Tactics That Win

As mentioned earlier, the curriculum is based on the Harvard case study approach, and is therefore focused on tracing significant corporate events and transactions in intensive detail. Often these sweeping narratives are less compelling to the graduates than the tactics and lessons that they learn from them.

This real-world perspective is exemplified by the questions most commonly asked after analyzing a typical case study:

- How does the CEO succeed at the negotiating table?
- What unique skills and strategies does she employ?
- Is there a blueprint I can use for conducting *my* negotiations?

Managing a business unit, and in the process advancing a career, involves overcoming a continuous series of challenges. The most successful managers recognize early on that standard approaches are rarely the most effective. By utilizing innovative ways of thinking, these flexible managers are able to identify and leverage a competitive advantage. Revelations like this that serve as vital management weapons are some of the greatest lessons of the AMP program.

This next section helps you explore a series of management options. It focuses on innovations, both simple and complex, that can help build an organization that has greater energy, creativity, and financial performance than the sum of its parts. The idea is to take what may be viewed as routine problems and challenges with prescribed solutions and view them through a prism that opens new perspectives and opportunities for action.

QUALITY IS GOOD—STRATEGY IS BETTER

Ask business managers to define quality and they'll talk about fit and finish, zero defects and superior workmanship. But this limited view fails to reflect the greater truth that quality is actually strategy.

Japan's penetration of the U.S. luxury car market in the 1980s and early 1990s is a clear example of engineering and marketing prowess unleashed as a daunting competitive force in global markets. Almost overnight, Acura/Lexus/Infiniti took major chunks of market share by engineering a new breed of well-

Mark Stevens

designed, meticulously manufactured, and competitively priced upscale automobiles.

As the following data from the J.D. Power and Associates Quality Survey demonstrates, the Japanese claimed seven of the top ten spots on the quality hit parade.

AUTOMOBILE QUALITY			
1990 Rank	1989 Rank	Brand	Defects Per 100 Cars
1	N/A	Lexus	82
2	2	Mercedes-Benz	84
3	1	Toyota	89
4	N/A	Infiniti	99
5	7	Buick	113
6	5	Honda	114
7	4	Nissan	123
8	6	Acura	129
9	19	BMW	139
9	8	Mazda	139

Much like other automakers, BMW's global management team feared Japan's encroachment into the luxury market. They recognized the tremendous threat inherent in Tokyo's market-leading price-quality ratio. Clearly, no one could match the Japanese in building nearly flawless automobiles at highly competitive prices. But as much as the Germans admitted the power of the Japanese threat, they saw no reason to succumb to it. Using the most effective competitive tool of all—an ingenious strategy—they set out to defend their position.

As BMW analyzed its position in the face of the Japanese onslaught, management recognized that their competitors' strategy was to excel at a facet of quality known as conformance. This meant that every automobile part and mechanical system was built and installed to within 99.99999 percent of engineering and manufacturing specifications. Bottom line: Virtually zero defects. Zero variance. A Swiss watch on wheels.

Admirable, said the folks at BMW . . . And impossible to beat if they tried to fine-tune the quality standard from 99.99999 to 100 percent. But because the Germans recognized that quality is perceived in many ways, the BMW team set out on a far more promising track. They decided to base BMW's approach on a strategy that would highlight *performance* as the key element of its *quality* standard.

BMW's Legacy of Performance

To place this all in context, it is important to understand the modern BMW's high-performance legacy. Founded in 1916 by Gustav Otto, the son of a pioneer of the internal combustion engine, Bayerische Motoren Werke, BMW, began as a producer of aircraft engines.

When the company began producing cars in the

late 1920s, sport racing competition enabled BMW's engineers to experiment with numerous automotive innovations, including aerodynamic body styling, new suspension systems, and high-performance engines. Through success on the racetrack and the introduction of several trend-setting sporty roadsters, BMW built a reputation for high-performance engineering that has remained one of its key selling points over the years.

In addition to styling, heavy investments in research and development put the company at the leading edge of technology in such critical areas as engine power and proficiency, pollution control, safety chassis design, suspension systems, automotive electronics, and transmissions. Few other car companies in the world could match BMW in performance, handling, and safety. Automotive critics regularly voted BMW's models the best cars in the world in their respective classes. Juxtaposed on this background of advanced technology was a culture that prized the craft traditions of Europe. Skilled workers and technicians were still required to go through a rigorous three-year apprenticeship. BMW was proud of the apprenticeship program and the people it produced. As management liked to say, "They think in hundredths of millimeters. That's the foundation of our quality."

To counterattack the late 1980s Japanese assault, BMW refocused on its high-performance legacy. Acknowledging that its core customer placed a premium value on the driving experience, the German carmaker invested in features designed to simulate the sports car feel in luxury sedans. They succeeded impressively, producing redesigned BMWs that were a hit with consumers. This new game plan stalled Japan's market share juggernaut and reversed a BMW sales slump with sharp new growth in the U.S. market. The strategy of battling conformance with performance secured a bull's-eye in the marketplace.

As you think about quality in your division or department, look at the big picture to address the strategy that will best guide your company in the marketplace. Only then can you define what quality means to you and your customers, and how it can help to achieve your business goals. Remember, quality is good, but a strategy that defines a specific aspect of quality designed to provide a competitive advantage, is better.

For AT&T executive and AMP graduate Carol Knauff, looking beyond the standard defects and bugs to her business, adopted a strategy that led her to install a quality improvement system that galvanized her business unit to compete more effectively for market share. Her process was built on an integrated approach that stressed attention to detail and incorporated competitive benchmarking, evaluation, and improvement—all combined in an interactive process with her team members and customers.

"I demonstrated my resolve to elevate my unit's quality standards by bringing in specialists with full authority to create a quality measurement system," says Knauff. "To drive responsibility for the quality process throughout our ranks, I assessed individual contributions to the quality process as part of every employee's periodic reviews. I did this in two phases. First, as we set out to build a quality measurement system, I rated my people on the progress they were making in getting this done. Everyone had a timeline, and how effective they were in conforming to that schedule became the initial method for measuring their contribution. Second, once the measurement was in place, I assessed people by the quality scores they received from their customers. This made it easy to identify performance on the quality improvement spectrum manager by manager.

"The quality specialists I brought in built a measurement methodology that ranked us against the competition and provided a mechanism for tracking our progress both independently and in comparison to industrywide best practices.

"The measurement system was called Customer Value Added. It's a rather complex mechanism, but it boils down to this acid test: Does the customer believe that what they purchased is worth the price they paid for it? If so, the system then ranks the attributes that caused the customer to reach that conclusion.

"For example, we ask the customer such questions as:

- "Are our people courteous?
- "Do they demonstrate high levels of product knowledge?
- "Do we accomplish all that you expect in a single service call?

"By assessing this feedback, and weighing it in the context of overall customer ratings of our product and service quality, we were able to identify the key drivers of high quality ratings in our business. Then we compared all this data to our competitors' satisfaction levels. Armed with this information, we knew precisely where to focus our efforts as we worked to move the needle on our quality rating. This enabled us to be highly targeted and efficient as we moved up the quality improvement curve. Clearly, the measurement system provided a valuable tool for building our customer relationships.

"Our progress proved to be doubly rewarding. As we measured higher in terms of product and service quality relative to our competition, we discovered that there was a direct correlation between quality and market share. When our quality ratings rose, our market share rose in tandem. This reinforced the key point that quality improvement is integral to running a business the smart way."

Knauff's AMP experience, combined with the pragmatic application of strategies and tactics she learned there, have led her to Three Rules for Managing Quality:

1. Senior management must be completely involved in the process rather than simply supportive of it. This means they must be willing to allow for independent assessment of the company's product and service quality, accept the findings, and act on them.
2. The quality focus must be endemic throughout the corporation or business unit, not simply the mission of an ancillary group or committee.
3. Quality improvement must be measured both in quality-specific terms and in terms of the impact it has on macro and micro business goals.

In the Art and Science of Negotiating, the Heavyweights Start at the End and Work Backward

Just how well an organization functions as a competitive unit is often evidenced by how well it performs in negotiations. It's important to understand this principle with an eye toward discovering why the successful negotiators win, how you can identify and adopt their strategies and tactics, and how to introduce their winning ways to your corporate culture.

We all assume the role of negotiator at one time or another. Whether you're negotiating a better price for your company's product or wrangling for a raise, you're negotiating. Whatever prize is at stake, you're likely to enter the negotiations focused on what you want and determined to convince your adversaries that you deserve it.

That's a common approach, but it's not how Bill Gates, Donald Trump, and Henry Kissinger negotiate. Eschewing the shoot-first-for-my-gain approach, they move their point of view to the other side of the table. They ask themselves at the outset what their adversaries want to achieve. They then craft a strategy creating the illusion that their opponents are winning the negotiation but in reality they come out on top.

In this context, the point-counterpoint that ricochets across the negotiating table is a sideshow, one that distracts the untutored and leaves them vulnerable to the skilled strategist's master plan.

The first lesson to learn is that when tactfully employed, compromise is a strength, not a weakness.

"The Advanced Management Program's elective on negotiating prompted me to recognize that when companies don't come to an agreement in a negotiation, they are not simply failing to agree—they are flunking out," says AMP graduate Oey Meesook, country director, World Bank. "They paint themselves into opposite corners and look at each other from across the room, paralyzed. In this nowhere situation it's easy to point fingers at the other side and hold your ground, but that means you're simply admitting to failure.

"The Harvard experience taught me ways to avoid this stalemate. Now, when I'm in the midst of tough negotiations, I think about one of the AMP cases where a number of parties were seeking to resolve a complex dispute. For every successful move they made, they would win points. The idea was that everyone would come away from the negotiations with measurable points or benefits—unless the parties failed to reach any kind of agreement. In that event, all points were eliminated. This made me see that unless I am willing to compromise, and can use my skills to get others to do the same, we will all flunk out. This is something we know instinctively, but in the heat of negotiations, emotions get in the way. When you break the negotiations down to component parts, and bear in mind the idea that no agreement equals no points, you can cut through the emotions and be highly pragmatic.

"The big point is that I have to use my skills not to vanquish my opponent, but instead to foster compromise that will allow all sides to walk away with points."

The second lesson is that recognizing the right points on which to compromise is equally essential.

In most negotiations, the tough decisions run along a fault line that is fraught with financial consequences for both sides. AT&T vice president Kathryn Anderson employs a battle strategy designed to create a smart framework for guiding one's actions in such a setting.

"At AMP I learned to boil down the hundred and one issues that are likely to arise in the course of a negotiation to the half dozen key drivers that are most important to my side and another half dozen that are likely to be of paramount importance to our adversaries," says Anderson. "I put dollar values on these critical issues and create spreadsheets that reveal the impact of making concessions on any given point. Then, I have my team prepare cheat sheets with this information for the negotiating sessions. This gives us a powerful advantage. As the give-and-take proceeds, we know the precise impact, in dollars and cents, of the points we win or concessions we choose to make. And because we have already isolated the key drivers on both sides of the table, we know where to focus our efforts through every minute of the negotiations. In effect, we can make highly informed decisions, apprised of all implications, on a real-time basis.

"My team used this approach in an $80 million negotiation and it worked superbly. Because we had plotted out the opposition's key drivers, we knew something was askew when they veered from these points during the negotiations. Most important, we offered them a concession that our calculations indicated would be worth a lot of money to them. But they blew it off as if it were meaningless. This prompted us to look for ancillary factors that could be influencing their approach. The cheat sheet sensitized us to what turned out to be strange behavior on the part of our opponents. In the course of this due diligence, we found that their team was being distracted by major political factors within their company. Learning why this was happening, and the direction it was pushing our adversaries, put us in a strong negotiating position. It's possible that we would have known something was askew without the benefit of the cheat sheets, but as it was, the fact that something big was going on behind the scenes came screaming off the page at us. We won because we studied our adversaries, knew what they needed to claim victory and what it would cost us to give them this illusion while we walked away with the prize."

An interview with Harvard Business School professor Jay O. Light:

Q. As the professor who teaches the AMP elective for negotiating, what do you believe is the most critical mistake businesspeople make when they go into a negotiating session?

A. That they personalize the process and get their egos wrapped up in it. I can't tell you how many times I hear them say, "If the other guy thinks he can get the best of me, he has another thing coming. When it comes to negotiating, I'm not one to mess around with. The other guy will learn soon enough that I don't crack easily and that when I want something, I get it."

This kind of attitude isn't negotiating, it's arm wrestling, and anyone can play that kind of macho game. Truth is, if you go into negotiations thinking first and foremost that you want the biggest piece of the pie, in all likelihood you're going to lose.

Q. That sounds rather Pollyannaish. Would you want the smaller piece of the pie?

A. Of course not. But what you're missing is that what you get is all a matter of perspective and approach. Rather than thinking only that you want the biggest piece of the pie, it is better to think, How can I expand the pie for both sides and then get the share that I want? A good example is a classic negotiation scenario we use as a teaching tool at the business school. It simulates a real-life negotiation between an aerospace contractor and a foreign government. In this case, the government is that of an oil-producing nation. By engaging in a series of nonlinear trade-offs—such as providing jet fighters in return for petroleum production in addition to cash—the contractor discovers it can create a greater opportunity for both sides. It's the perfect example of thinking of ways to enlarge the pie before you cut your piece.

Q. What are some of the other strategies of successful negotiators?

A. The great negotiators realize that once they are in the room it is too late to prepare. Assume you are involved in a multiparty negotiation with four, five, or six parties, vying to achieve a certain goal. A skilled negotiator will use the time to build coalitions with some of the others before they all sit down across the table from one another. A less effective negotiator will completely overlook this extremely important part of the process.

One of our negotiation exercises has to do with building a port. As the exercise unfolds, it becomes clear that if parties are smart enough to work in advance to build a strong coalition with several of the others engaged in the negotiations, they get a superior agreement. When the others see how they've been outfoxed, they often turn around and say, "Ah-ha, I see what I did wrong. I failed to build a coalition at the outset. In other words, I failed to see all the possibilities and address them in advance."

WAR GAMES MAKE YOUR BUSINESS BATTLE-READY

At any time competition can blindside you. Competitors can penetrate your customer base, recruit distributors, or erode your leadership in technology, pricing, innovation, or quality. Suddenly, the strengths and assets you take for granted are vulnerable and incapable of protecting your market share.

Once you are in this position your options are limited. Weakened by the competitive assault, and forced to protect against further encroachment, you are pressed to act quickly, often forced to opt for speed over carefully constructed strategy. In this context mistakes—and the negative consequences they bring—are likely to multiply.

The best way to avoid this scenario is to conduct simulated war games that seek to anticipate competitive tactics and help you craft a powerful response to them. This makes your business battle-ready and prepared to face a wide range of contingencies.

War games can be used as an effective component of the strategic planning process. For example, when Toyota's management is planning its products, pricing, and advertising for the next three years, it would be helpful to anticipate Honda's, General Motors', and BMW's strategies over the same period. The war games exercise makes it possible to peer into the future, envision a wide range of competitive scenarios, and prepare for them.

The AMP war games approach for crafting a bulletproof strategy starts by seeking answers to four questions:

1. Is the competition satisfied with its current position?
2. What will the competition do to achieve satisfaction?
3. When is the competition most vulnerable?
4. What moves on your part will likely prompt competitive retaliation?

This analysis provides important insight into what the battlefield looks like now and what the battlefield may look like under a likely set of competitive scenarios.

"To bring these pictures into focus, companies should go off-site for war game maneuvers," says Professor Earl Sasser. "It works this way: Company A divides its war games managers into commanders of Company A, as well as officers of competitors B, C, and D. The competition then attacks A with questions and challenges designed to identify A's Achilles' heel. In effect, collective intelligence is applied to uncover hidden vulnerabilities with the goal of taking corrective action that will fortify A's competitive position.

"This process can replicate A's competitive environment. For example, there is an information technology consulting firm we'll call XYZ Co. that often wins and loses customers on the basis of written proposals and in-person presentations. XYZ and its competitors serve up their best sales pitches and hope to walk away with a contract to create products or deliver services.

"Determined to improve its batting average in the new business pitches, XYZ's management simulated this bake-off process at a war games retreat designed to turn the company's executives into its own worst critics. The way the games were structured, management was divided into groups representing the host company and its competitors. All groups were presented with a new business opportunity and were required to prepare proposals designed to win the potential customer's business. Once completed, all proposals were reviewed and rated by a panel of judges, blind to the identity of the presenters.

"When the verdict came in the judges ranked the host company's proposal—created by its real-world proposal team—dead last. This prompted management to review and redesign its proposal process and to replace members of the proposal team."

The key point here is that war games can simulate the competitive environment, identify weaknesses, and enable your company to make critical changes that produce a more complete and effective competitive strategy that ultimately leads to a higher win ratio in the marketplace.

LEVERAGING THE POWER OF CRITICAL OPPOSITES

As managers make the transition from war games to real-world battles, they must identify and incorporate a strategic advantage. AMP professor Michael Beer believes this can be found in an organizational and cultural context that seeks to leverage, rather than diminish, opposing forces.

"In today's corporate environment a manager earns respect by demonstrating a determination to engage the organization forcefully enough to achieve its objectives," Beer says. "This requires flexibility and courage as opposed to brute force. The leader must be equally strong in confronting the obstacles to success when they are identified in superiors, subordinates, the corporate structure, or his or her own shortcomings.

"Effective leadership demands a delicate balance between sensitivity and authority. However, many managers fail to establish sufficient balance to make the equation work. They operate under the wrong internal message, which tells them to be either laissez-faire or overly controlling. Let's see where this breaks down. The laissez-faire manager—isolated, detached, and benign—creates more problems for herself and the business than the autocrat she is determined not to be. She may pride herself on her willingness to grant employees carte blanche empowerment. Her directive to subordinates might be to assess the issues . . . make decisions . . . stick by them.

"But by tilting too far toward a majority vote democracy, the manager becomes reluctant to exercise sufficient force necessary to propel the company toward its goals. This creates an organization bereft of leadership. In such an environment, management fails to coordinate the various components of the enterprise and, in turn, fails to harness the positive factors inherent in the conflict between operating units (such as credit versus sales or technology versus human resources). Ironically, what appears to authorize an exceptional level of personal freedom and flexibility turns out to be a trap. Call it the paradox of empowerment.

"People need to operate within a framework of boundaries and ground rules," Professor Beer adds. "This provides a context for mobilizing their skills and energies in pursuit of personal and collective goals. Unless they are made aware of their operating parameters at the outset, they are bound to make mistakes, exceed their authority, and be rebuked for it. Inevitably, this leads to fear, confusion, and insecurity. Caught in the headlights, they become paralyzed."

An important but widely overlooked principle of business success is that integrating opposites, as opposed to identifying them as inconsistencies and driving them out, unleashes power. This is true on both a personal level (the balanced manager is more effective than his or her peer at one end of the control spectrum) and on an organizational level as well.

The fact is, managers tend to create misleading dichotomies based on black and white statements that appear to be mutually exclusive:

- A manager is either authoritarian or anarchistic.
- A company is either focused on its shareholders or dedicated to its employees.
- A business is either centralized or decentralized.

All of these statements are false. Furthermore, they all create barriers to sustained levels of superior corporate performance.

"On an organizational level we accept the existence of hard and fast dichotomies because this binary perspective helps to rationalize personal styles, viewpoints, cultures, and structures," Beer adds. "But this kind of polarized thinking is simplistic, misleading, and overlooks the fact that in the business world ideal approaches are generally painted in gray as opposed to black and white.

"To be successful in a complex and competitive world, you must embrace and manage critical opposites."

COMPETING THE HEWLETT-PACKARD WAY

To see how managing critical opposites plays out at an organizational level compare two dramatically different companies: Apple Computer and Hewlett-Packard. The former has fluctuated wildly; the latter has been a venerable performer. To identify why their paths have diverged this way, one can take the knee-jerk response of examining their respective technologies for relative strengths and weaknesses. But that would be misleading because the answer isn't about technology at all. Rather, Apple and HP were founded on dramatically disparate philosophies.

At Apple, technology—reflected in the form and function of Apple products—was at the center of the universe. The gospel according to Apple, particularly in its early years, before the return of founder Steve Jobs as CEO, held that technological innovations would be sufficiently powerful to create sustainable and competitive growth. For this reason proprietary technology was the key to corporate success and individual effort was secondary.

HP took a different tack. Founders David Packard and William Hewlett set out to create an organization that could sustain its competitive advantage regardless of marketplace whims and what their competitors were building. To accomplish this they based their corporate culture on the integration and reinforcement of critical opposites. This became known as the Hewlett-Packard Way.

Hewlett-Packard has achieved what appears to be the greatest dichotomy: creating an environment that celebrates individualism, but at the same time one that is also wholly supportive of teamwork. Interestingly, when the Japanese look at HP, they say this is a Japanese company. This stems from the Japanese focus on teamwork and on forging a highly developed collaborative workplace. In an Asian environment, the group supercedes the individual. Perhaps the most symbolic expression of this cultural phenomenon is revealed in the group prayer sessions that are often conducted on the factory floor at the start of a Japanese workday. But viewing the HP environment as a near clone of this style is not accurate. Although HP people are taught to engage in cross-functional teams, they are also rated on the performance of decentralized business units and personal achievement. Perhaps the most telling point is that while historically Japanese companies have been wedded to lifetime employment, if you underperform at HP you're out.

The failure to integrate critical opposites in the HP manner has taken a heavy toll on both American and Japanese companies that have allowed either individualism or consensus building to be taken to the extreme. That's because single-mindedness always comes up short in a battle with multidimensional competitors.

In a related case example, the Japanese dominated the global automobile industry in the 1970s and 1980s in great measure because their team-oriented culture produced excellent quality implementation. But now that the quality gap has closed and technical innovation is increasingly important, the Japanese are forced to play catch-up. Their lack of experience in managing dualities—specifically in creating a delicate balance between teamwork and individual creativity—has turned out to be a liability they are hard-pressed to fix.

"Early in our history while thinking about how a company like this should be managed, I kept getting back to one concept," said David Packard. "If we could simply get everyone to agree on that one objective and to understand what we were trying to do we could turn everybody loose, and they would move along in a common direction."

From the start, these corporate objectives were set in the framework of a value system meant to establish standards for HP employees in dealing with their co-workers and customers. Originally put in writing in 1989 by David Packard, these values—the centerpiece of the Hewlett-Packard Way—are as follows (Beer and Rogers 1995):

- We approach each situation with the belief that people want to do a good job and will do so, given the proper tools and support. We attract highly capable, diverse, and innovative people and recognize their efforts and contributions to the company.
- Our customers expect HP products and services to be of the highest quality and to provide lasting value. To achieve this, all HP people—but especially managers—must be leaders who generate enthusiasm and respond with extra effort to meet customer needs.
- We expect HP people to be open and honest in their dealings, so as to earn the trust and loyalty of others. People at every level are expected to adhere to the highest standards of business ethics and must understand that anything less is totally unacceptable.
- We recognize that it is only through effective cooperation within and among the organizations that we can achieve our goals.
- We create an inclusive work environment that supports the diversity of our people and stimulates innovation. We allow people flexibility in working toward goals in ways that they help determine are best for the organization.

Most companies tend to recruit, train, and promote people within functional silos. But HP breaks down the walls, creating a career maze that begins with the recruitment of a diverse workforce (based on personality and skills, not simply gender and ethnicity) and then promotes horizontally, as well as vertically, throughout the company. Typically, HP employees move through four to six functional areas in the course of their careers. This creates broad knowledge of the company and fosters the kind of teamwork other companies covet. One of the company's managers sums it up best: "There is no prescribed career development or progression pattern. In a lot of companies, you can sit down and do a flow chart. If you want to get to point F, you do A, then B, then C, then D, and E, and you're ready for F. You can describe each job. It's not true in this company. When it comes time to promote, we try to look for the best people. There are many paths you can follow to any particular end. It's not necessary to get a bigger title or to jump a level in the pay system to be given new responsibility."

AMP professor Michael Beer sums up succinctly the reasons for Hewlett-Packard's success in a highly competitive business environment:

"You can't achieve what HP has accomplished by writing provisions on a mission statement. . . . A mission statement is an espousal of what you'd like to be. The only way you can become what you're saying you'd like to be is to test whether people perceive the way you're leading and managing the organization as being consistent with the espoused mission statement. Embedded in that is the idea that the mission statement reflects the leaders' own strongly held values. If the leaders come to realize that their behavior is inconsistent with what they're espousing, they must be willing to change or move over and let somebody else take over. That's the only way I know to effectively change an organization."

THE POWER OF ORGANIZATIONAL STRATEGY: MASTERING THE 7-S MODEL

As a business manager, you are in many ways an organizational architect. You need blueprints for assembling and integrating the varied components of your organization and for driving them toward your strategic goals and objectives. With this in mind, imagine you are seeking a competitive advantage by being the industry leader in customer service. You will face a series of challenges:

- How do you motivate people to provide a high caliber of service?
- How do you structure compensation to reflect an employee's impact on client satisfaction?
- Should you invest in customer service training programs?
- Are you best advised to limit new recruits to those with a customer service orientation?

To complicate matters, assume the business unit has multiple offices:

- How do you manage and coordinate the facilities to assure a uniform standard of service?
- How do you guide the head of each office to be entrepreneurial in exploiting local opportunities while working together to pursue global interests?
- What shared values, reporting structures, and information systems are required to achieve your goals?

In short, how do you begin to best organize and manage your company for competitive advantage? One school of research has culminated in the 7-S model, a tool for managerial analysis and action developed by a team of professors from Harvard and Stanford business schools and consultants from McKinsey & Company (Bradach 1996).

This model holds that seven key elements of an organization are critical to understanding its effectiveness: strategy, structure, systems, staffing, skills, style, and shared values. To be effective, an organization must have a high degree of fit, or internal alignment, among these seven elements. That is, each S must be consistent with and reinforce the other S's.

Strategy is best thought of as a plan an organization formulates to gain a sustainable advantage over the competition. Sample strategies might be to:

- Compete on cost.
- Deliver greater value to customers.
- Provide distinctive product features.
- Develop innovative sales and service approaches.

Boiled down to its essence, strategy is, or ought to be, an organization's way of saying, "Here is our unique selling proposition."

Questions to ask about your company's strategy include:

- What are the sources of sustainable competitive advantage (cost, quality, service, technical leadership, and so forth)?
- What are the key strategic priorities (for example, penetrating new markets, new product development, speed to market, improved customer service)?

Structure refers to the framework in which the activities of the organization's members are coordinated. A key function of structure is to focus employees' attention on what needs to get done by defining the work they do and whom they should be working with. One significant challenge leaders face is balancing the need for specialization with the need for integration. For example, a common problem in the product development process is a lack of proper coordination between people working in manufacturing, design, and marketing. Structure helps overcome this problem as well as others.

There are four basic structural forms—functional, divisional, matrix, and network.

In the most common arrangement—the functional form—an individual is placed in charge of each major activity that must be accomplished for the organization to carry out its business. Typically someone heads up manufacturing and someone else is responsible for sales—and both report to the president. This form works well in a small organization facing a relatively stable environment where coordination across functions is not yet critical. While separate departments help to develop deep knowledge in each functional area, they also make it difficult to coordinate activities across departmental boundaries. Organizations often establish cross-functional teams to deal with this dilemma.

In the divisional structure diverse functions are grouped into divisions that may be organized by product, geography, or market segment. Each division contains all the needed functions, such as manufacturing, marketing research, and development. Corporate headquarters is responsible for allocating resources to each division, coordinating activities across the units, and setting the long-term strategy. Given that each division has all the necessary resources on hand, this structure enables each major unit of the business to react quickly and effectively to threats and opportunities related to its product, market, or geographic region.

On the other hand, divisional structure has two significant disadvantages. Because each division possesses its own resources, there is wasteful duplication and a failure to harness economies of scale. Also, coordination across divisions can be difficult and costly. For example, salespeople from different divisions may call upon the same customer, creating potential confusion and dissatisfaction.

The matrix structure attempts to harness the best of both the functional and divisional structures. Both functional and divisional managers have equal authority within the organization and employees report to both of them. This can provide the advantage of functional expertise and divisional autonomy. However, matrix structures often generate high levels of conflict and ambiguity because it may not be clear who is in control and accountable. For a matrix to work, managers must develop mutual trust, expectations, and influence.

The network structure has gained prominence in the last decade. Network structures vary, but they also share a few characteristics. First, the network is composed of relatively small semiautonomous groups that either temporarily or permanently join with other groups to achieve common objectives (project teams, for example).

Second, the boundaries are porous between the organization and its environment. Partnerships with vendors and customers, and other such relationships, blur what is inside and outside the organization.

Third, authority tends to be based more on one's expertise and resources than on one's formal position. The main advantage of the network structure is that it can fluidly adapt and reconfigure itself in times of rapid change.

Organizations often adopt variations of these basic structural forms. The key issue for leaders to understand is that the structure chosen can lead people to focus attention on certain issues and ignore others. Plus, the chosen structure can greatly influence which organizational subunits have the most power and influence.

Questions you might ask about your company's structure include:

- What is its basic form?
- How centralized or decentralized is the organization?

- What is the relative status and power of the organizational subunits?

Systems have a profound impact on organizational effectiveness because they focus the attention of managers. Consider the fact that many organizations are introducing cross-functional teams. One of the biggest impediments to this team approach is a traditional compensation system that rewards people on individual as opposed to collective or collaborative performance.

Similarly, consider efforts to reengineer companies. These initiatives create processes that cut across conventional organizational boundaries. A successful reengineering effort almost always involves an overhaul of the existing systems to support the new flow of work—compensation systems, management information systems, and capital allocation systems.

Questions to ask about your company's systems:

- Does the organization have the systems it needs to run your business? (For example, does it have a system for monitoring customer satisfaction?)
- What are the systems that management uses to run the company?
- Which ones are given priority attention?

Staffing refers to how people are developed, specifically, how recruits are trained, socialized, integrated, and ultimately how their careers are managed. One of the most common sayings in business is, "People are our most important asset." If this is true, organizational effectiveness is largely determined by who the people are and how the organization develops them. High-performance companies pay extraordinary attention to recruiting the right people into the organization and providing them with the training and opportunities needed to develop their potential (Pfeffer 1994).

Questions to ask about your company's staffing:

- How does the organization recruit and develop people (formal training and mentoring programs)?
- What are the demographic characteristics of the management team (background, education, age, gender, nationality, professional identity, experience outside the company)?
- Where are the strongest leaders found in the organization (in which functions)? Where are the weakest?

Skills are the distinctive competencies—people, management practices, systems, and/or technology—that reside in the organization. Observers often characterize skills as what the company does best.

Skills represent an opportunity to the extent that they can be applied to new markets. For example, 3M has applied its innovative adhesive products to a variety of markets. However, skills such as these may also act as a constraint when a new and different set of skills are required to compete—either because the market has shifted its priorities (from quality to cost, for example) or the firm seeks to enter new business arenas. In this case, the firm may need to learn new skills and unlearn old skills.*

---

*For a discussion of how learning new skills and unlearning old ones affects a firm's ability to innovate, see Leonard-Barton (1992).

Questions to ask about your company's skills:

- What business activities is the company distinctively good at performing?
- What new capabilities does the company need to develop, and which ones does it need to unlearn to compete in the future?

Style is the leadership approach of top management, and the organization's overall operating approach. Although style may be set largely by one or two leaders of the organization, it is used here to refer to the overall behavior patterns of management team members. For example, how do managers spend their time (in meetings versus walking around the office)? Where do they focus their attention (inside the firm versus outside)?

Some questions to ask about your company's style:

- How does top management make decisions (for example, participatory versus top-down, analytic versus armchair)?
- Where do managers focus their time and attention (in formal meetings, informal conversations, in the field, with customers, in the lab)?

Shared values are the core set of values that serve as the guiding principles of the organization. These values go beyond the formal statement of corporate objectives found in the company's policy book, to what is truly important to people in the organization. Shared values provide stability amid what is often a shifting set of internal and external dynamics.

Questions to ask about your company's shared values:

- Do people have a shared understanding of why the company exists?
- Do people have a shared understanding of the company's vision?
- What types of issues receive the most and least top management attention (for example, short-run versus long-run, internal versus external)?
- How do people describe the ways in which the company is distinctive (focus on quality, emphasis on people)?

Shared values are one of the most important elements of an organization's culture. For discussions of culture, see Hill (1998). For a more detailed discussion of shared values and vision, see Kotter (1990) and Collins and Porras (1996).

Identifying Opportunities for Improvement: Using the 7-S Model

Leaders and consultants often use the 7-S model to help get their arms around the complex problem of capturing the factors that shape an organization's behavior and performance. The underlying theory of the model is simple. When different parts of an organization are poorly aligned, the organization will often exhibit problems and perform below its potential. When they are well aligned, the company often leverages the power of synergy and achieves exceptional performance.

Using the model to diagnose problems in an organization involves analyzing the degree of fit between each of the seven S's. For example:

- Does the staffing process support the distinctive skills the organization is trying to develop?
- Does the structure fit the strategy the firm is pursuing?

Below are two examples of misalignment:

- A retail firm's strategy is to compete on the basis of delivering superior service to customers. However, its managers are rewarded entirely for meeting their budget targets. This top-down style of management inhibits the local decision making needed for delivering exceptional service.
- An investment bank seeks to build broad and deep relationships with clients by offering them a full line of products (cash management, fixed income, trading, and so on), but the bank's reward system is based entirely on the performance of individual departments, not the overall firm. Further, the bank is staffed with people with vast technical expertise, but little skill managing relationships inside or outside the firm.

In both of these cases a 7-S analysis would serve to highlight areas that might limit each company's effectiveness. Organizations must also stay aligned with their external environment (product and labor markets, sociopolitical boundaries, and so on). The most common external problems occur when organizations pursue strategies and align the other six S's accordingly so that they are no longer viable in the competitive environment. An organization perfectly aligned to compete with a strategy based on product differentiation, for instance, will need to adapt its strategy and the other S's if the purchase criterion of its customers shifts to price.

When faced with a problem in the performance of an organization, a leader needs to identify the possible areas of misalignment, analyze why they have occurred, and begin to explore ideas for correcting the problems.

Managing Change with the 7-S Model

Consider the following when using the 7-S model as a tool for proposing and evaluating plans for changing an organization:

- All seven variables are interconnected. It is often difficult to make progress on one without making adjustments to the others as well. A failed organizational change effort is often the result of not recognizing the role played by all of the S's.
- The model does not imply any natural starting point for a change effort. There is no assumption that one S has more impact on effectiveness than any other S. In some cases, the critical variable might be staffing. In others, it could be that the systems or structures are impeding the implementation of the strategy. Only by going through a diagnosis of the alignment of the organization can you determine where you need to focus your attention.
- While a thorough diagnosis may point to the need to change any one of the S's, each one differs in

how easily and directly it can be changed. Most analysts agree that strategy, structure, and systems—what are referred to as the "hard S's"—are easier to change than the others. Indeed, leaders often begin change efforts by altering one or more of these hard S's. The "softer S's"—staffing, skills, style, and shared values—are harder to change directly, and typically take longer to do so, but research suggests that effective companies tend to pay as much attention to these factors as to the hard S's.

How to Pick and Manage Markets Competitors Can't Penetrate

Ask Michael Dell, Bill Gates, and Wayne Huizenga and they'll all confirm the axiom: Build a better mousetrap and the world will beat a path to your door. But bringing hot new products to market also carries an abundance of risk. No sooner does the world come knocking at your door than competitors are vying for a share of your market by offering more efficient and attractive mousetraps at a lower cost. Suddenly, your market lead erodes.

This scenario plays out in hundreds of domestic and international markets. Managers generally accept it as an inevitable by-product of economic Darwinism. But there is a corridor of opportunity lying beneath the surface that offers superior companies the ability to shield against the onslaught of competition by producing exceptional returns over protracted periods.

When Crown Cork and Seal's CEO John Connelly searched for a low-risk, high-reward strategy for penetrating global markets relatively free of competition, he hit upon the innovative idea of negotiating pioneer rights with developing nations. In return for establishing industrial beachheads in these countries, often with obsolete equipment recycled from U.S. plants, Crown Cork was granted first rights to produce its core products—tin cans and bottle caps—in a series of emerging markets. With this shrewd stroke, Crown Cork gained a monopoly in the marketplace. By the time Connelly, hailed as a Johnny Appleseed of the global marketplace, retired in 1989, Crown Cork's sixty-two overseas facilities produced a 54 percent increase of the company's operating profits.

"Great companies generate returns substantially in excess of their capital costs," says Advanced Management Program professor William E. Fruhan, Jr. "In many cases, they do it by creating barriers to entry. This takes the form of a tangible advantage that blocks competitors from successfully encroaching on your customer base. In such cases competitors are reluctant to challenge your lead, or, if they try, are hardpressed to make significant inroads in your market domination. Bottom line: Sales and margins remain strong and earnings far exceed the cost of capital."

Sustaining Competitive Advantage, Bill Gates Style

Historically, businesspeople have thought of scarcity as a competitive advantage. But in many industries today, ubiquity creates the sustainable advantage. In other words, more is really more.

In a sector such as technology, the rule of absolute numbers applies. Put simply, you can be a billion-dollar company, but your user base can still be relatively small (for example, Apple's technology versus the Windows/Intel user base).

In cases like this, one of Bill Gates's favorite concepts, network externality, comes into play. This holds that the value of a product increases with the size of its installed base. If there is only one telephone in the world, it has virtually no value. Double this to two phones and the value meter barely budges. Increase the number of telephones significantly and you have an explosion of use that leads to related products and vastly increased value. This is also the secret to Intel's sustainable advantage over Apple and illuminates a key point that can help corporate executives and entrepreneurs increase their effectiveness in building companies, departments, and careers.

Any business that considers itself strong and successful in its market still must pursue even greater growth on a faster track to achieve a sustainable competitive advantage.

Harvard Business School professor Michael Porter offers guidelines on competition and strategy revealing industry dynamics for managers seeking to enter new markets. Porter suggests that managers exploring broader landscapes should assess five revealing market dynamics:

- What is happening with buyers?
- What is happening with suppliers?
- What is happening with new entrants?

- What is happening with product or service substitutes?
- What is happening with rivalry among competitors?

Based on Porter's analysis, managers can rate industry attractiveness according to the following factors:

INDUSTRY ATTRACTIVENESS SCORECARD

- If the suppliers are few and powerful, the industry is not attractive.
- If there are a substantial number of new entrants, the industry is not attractive.
- If product or service substitutes are plentiful, the industry is not attractive.
- If there is intensive rivalry among existing players, the industry is not attractive.
- If the buyers are few and powerful, the industry is not attractive.

Porter's research indicates that in any market there are basically two ways to prosper: have a strong differentiation strategy or be a low-cost producer. Increasing market leaders, and successful new entrants into markets, make clear choices in their strategy. Southwest Airlines—which achieves low cost and low fares by sacrificing meals, assigned seats, and other amenities—is a good example. It made clear trade-offs that allowed it to distance itself from its rivals.

While the financial performance of Southwest's competitors is rocked by the airline industry's rises and dips, Southwest reports an unbroken streak of profits. Southwest makes it look easy. When it first invaded United Airlines' plum West Coast markets, Chicago-based United (rich, global, and self-assured) set out to beat Southwest at its own game.

United's management team identified three key components to Southwest's formula for success:

1. By relying on a single aircraft model, the stalwart Boeing 737, Southwest reduced maintenance, parts, and fuel costs.
2. By using a point-to-point route map instead of the hub-and-spoke system, Southwest reduced crew sizes and simplified logistics.
3. By building its presence at secondary airports, as opposed to the major urban fields, Southwest reduced airport charges and limited time between takeoffs and landings.

It was an apparently easy formula for United to replicate, which it attempted to do, at a cost of approximately $500 million. But just as United sat back and prepared to count the profits as it retaliated against Southwest, the venture collapsed amidst massive losses.

United's postmortem revealed the causes of this fiasco: The airline's due diligence had failed to identify the invisible factor that propelled Southwest from a fledgling carrier to a competitive juggernaut. By focusing on related activities, and building a team infused with a powerful esprit de corps, Southwest CEO Herb Kelleher had created a dynamic synergy among employees, technology, and systems.

United's turnaround time to land a plane, discharge

passengers, and take flight once again never broke the thirty-minute barrier. Yet Southwest—servicing the same planes at the same airports with the same number in its maintenance crew—routinely accomplishes this fundamental airline routine in less than half that time.

Southwest has proliferated competitive advantages throughout its value chain, including an exceptionally motivated workforce. Kelleher's commitment to the rank and file and his determination to ask questions, provide answers, and use every viable means to demonstrate the importance of employees has unleashed exceptional loyalty, extra effort, team spirit, and productivity that is the hallmark and a powerful asset of Southwest. Put simply, the companywide will to win fuels Southwest's success.

A fifteen-minute disparity in airplane turnaround time may seem inconsequential, but multiply that advantage by hundreds of turnarounds at scores of airports daily, and it means Southwest flies more flights with less equipment, thereby collecting more revenue. And so Southwest reigns as the airline industry's low-fare leader.

An interview with AMP professor William Fruhan on barriers to entry:

Q. The Southwest Airlines, Crown Cork, and Microsoft cases are valuable models for managers of big companies or their business units. But how can smaller players—like the president of a regional business equipment distribution company—create barriers to entry?

A. Fundamentally, there are two kinds of barriers. At

the high end, there are economies of scale, trade-marks, patents, trade secrets, and capital requirements. Each is a fundamental entry barrier that allows you to build in some protection from competitive entry in your market and, due to less competition, earn additional returns. These are the bold-stroke, business-model-changing kinds of activities. But there are also what I describe as the little quality of management issues. Every business has twenty variables that, if you get half of them right, will give you a 15 percent return. And if you get all twenty right, will give you a 20 percent return. By paying attention to little quality of management issues you can increase your return without changing any of the bold-stroke fundamental dynamics I mentioned above.

When you're talking about your hypothetical regional office equipment distributor, and other more modest-sized businesses, you're focusing on those kinds of quality of management issues. You're not going to change the fundamental paradigm of competition within the industry, but you can make it harder for others to compete against you—which will bolster your margins.

Professor Fruhan's point about how quality of management issues can add up is important. Consider the barriers to entry created by Ethel Truly, vice president, Mississippi Chemical Corporation, AMP Class of 1996.

"I have always recognized the important role people play in a company, but I had never identified the fact that an intelligent and integrated human resources strategy is the only sustainable competitive advantage. AMP made me recognize that every other corporate asset can be bought or replicated virtually overnight, but competitors seeking to duplicate a well-trained, motivated, and committed workforce will need at least a decade to catch up. Exceptional cultures just can't be created with the wave of a wand—or a major infusion of capital.

"This lesson left me more determined than ever to create a workforce that would provide a competitive advantage. Fortunately, our workforce was already grounded in a strong work ethic and a history of technical innovation, but we would also have to be:

- Innovative in every aspect of our business;
- Customer-oriented;
- Adaptable to changes in markets, strategy, procedures, and equipment and other work tools.

"With this in mind, our management team evaluated the strengths and weaknesses of our workforce and therefore the gap between where we felt our workforce was and where it needed to be. We then implemented two major programs:

"*Management Training and Support:* We had never done a good job of supporting people we'd promoted to managerial posts. Instead, we would take the best people from the operating ranks and put them in supervisory positions, even though they had little or no experience, and possibly no skill, in managing others. In effect, we promoted them based on abilities that were not relevant to their new positions and then let them sink or swim on their own. No longer. Now, we are providing training on:

- Thinking strategically.
- Establishing priorities.
- Giving and receiving feedback.
- Developing communication skills.
- Conducting effective personal interviews.
- Conflict resolution.
- Understanding the full scope of company strategy, policies, and procedures (once the training began, we discovered how much of this is often a mystery to people).
- The use of computers, digital equipment, and other tools, including for people who might have considered themselves nonusers.

"We have created a centralized training function, hired a training manager for the first time, and devoted substantially more resources to education of all kinds.

"*Personal Development Program:* Evaluating employees has always been a part of our standard operating procedure. In typical fashion, the evaluations focused on an employee's performance to date (usually very recent performance) with a report card approach. We think we've adopted a better system by linking an employee's evaluation to a series of personal development options.

"First, we subject employees to a 360 degree evaluation—meaning we get appraisals from peers, superiors, subordinates, and customers. The system forces narrative feedback, comments on those workforce 'gap characteristics' identified by senior management, and specific examples. (Thus far, we have been able to train only exempt employees on this system, but our plan is to extend it to nonexempt employees, both to provide them with the benefits of the system and to complete the 360 degree evaluation for exempt employees.)

"Then, we produce an assessment of strengths and weaknesses for the employee. Soon afterward, the employee and his supervisor select between one and three areas of development to make the person a more effective and productive member of the workforce. We have people trained to assist the employee and supervisor in creating a written development plan with a schedule. Development tools may include such traditional learning methods as attending seminars and reading helpful materials, but the emphasis is on growth on the job. A development plan might include, for example, participating in a company activity that will allow strengthening of particular skills, leading a project team, working in a different area of the company on some basis, or even service in a community group in a capacity that will provide the experience sought. Instead of handing out report cards, we offer tools that can serve as springboards to personal improvement, career success, and a workforce that has the skills we believe to be essential for the company's competitiveness.

"Once these efforts were well under way, our CEO concluded that, if our strategy was to evolve effectively and intelligently on a timely basis, senior managers needed more time away from the front lines to think, contemplate, and plan. From this insight came a requirement that the senior staff spend four days a month away from the office in individual reading, planning, and reflection. Offices have been created for this purpose in a building we own apart from the headquarters site but convenient to it. We have also organized a library of thought-provoking books, of which my personal favorite is *Sun Tzu and the Art of Business*—a book about applying strategies of the ancient Chinese military theorist to modern business issues, with which I became familiar at AMP. In addition, senior management regularly meets off-site to think about new opportunities and directions for the company. Once a year, senior management and the board of directors meet off-site for an extended session at which strategy and other matters are explored in depth.

"Our goal is a continuous loop of training, assessment, and improvement at all levels for maintaining a culture of excellence, even as the world around us changes and requires new skills and strategies. Our efforts are paying off—we see improvement in many areas that should translate into a sustainable competitive advantage."

THE ART OF MAKING YOUR BUSINESS STAND OUT FROM THE CROWD

Companies like Microsoft and Nike create and maintain barriers to entry through innovation. There's a popular school of thought that suggests the potential to innovate depends on the nature of the industry. According to this thinking, mature businesses selling commodity-type products have little room for creativity and the powerful competitive advantage that can go with it.

This is a misconception. Even the most formulaic businesses will respond powerfully to creative input. In fact, these businesses can leverage innovation to outmaneuver rivals who are saddled with limited perspectives of their competitive options. This leads to an important point: It's not industries that impose barriers to exceptional growth but instead the tunnel-visioned managers who fail to differentiate themselves in the marketplace.

"Our company is in the petroleum refining business," says Paul Eisman, senior vice president, Ultramar Diamond Shamrock Corporation, AMP Class of 1996. "We take crude oil and turn it into gasoline. It's not glamorous or fast-growth, like biotech or information technology, but we still have to run it and run it well. So how do we generate the kind of substantial growth and return we need to serve our shareholders when our industry is filled with powerful competitors all selling more or less the same product? According to AMP, I could learn from the men and women who have achieved this feat under similar circumstances, building great companies during their tenure. These leaders guided companies that appeared to be immune to dramatic infusions of ideas, energy, and firepower, and yet transformed them into innovative and aggressive category leaders.

"When you study these companies to see how they gained a marketplace advantage through organizational structure and innovative product presentation, three common traits come into focus:

- "*Operational Excellence:* They make certain that all components of the business are linked on an operational basis. There is extensive communication and collaboration among people, departments, and management across all functions and disciplines. Anyone who runs a business, or any part of a business, knows this cross-pollination doesn't happen spontaneously. You have to create an environment that allows communication to become a way of life.

- *"Sense of Mission:* Simply getting the job done and collecting a paycheck isn't good enough. You and your people have to recognize that you're on a mission to distinguish your company from peer businesses who accept the notion that there is little they can do to distance themselves from the competition.

- *"Focus on Innovation:* The best companies recognize that in every business function—pricing, marketing, purchasing, manufacturing, distribution— the most apparent and obvious way of doing things is probably not the most efficient or productive approach. So they drill below the obvious until they come up with an innovative approach or methodology. That's how and when they discover the way to stand out from the competition.

"From my perspective, all of this boils down to leveraging the power of knowledge. Great companies keep learning how to do things better, and keep spreading that knowledge throughout their organizations. Since returning from AMP, I've sought to emulate that by setting up a system called cross-refinery learning. It is a way of spreading the best practices established at one of our refineries to all seven refineries in our system. A chat room on our Intranet facilitates this by providing a forum for our technical people to share new concepts and developments with each other.

"We may always be an oil refining business that lacks the glamour of other industries, but there's always a powerful and financially rewarding way to establish ourselves as a leader. We're focused on that."

ACTION PLAN FOR LEVERAGING THE POWER OF LEARNING

Learning from successful role models is an essential part of the Advanced Management Program curriculum and the Harvard Business School case method approach on which it is based. A number of students pointed to the lessons they learned by reading and discussing the thinking of John Browne, CEO of British Petroleum. A Cambridge-educated physicist, Browne is an unabashed enthusiast of the power of corporate learning. From his perspective, learning provides the catalyst and the intellectual resource to create a competitive advantage.

Here's Browne's action plan for competitive learning:

- Anyone in the company who is not directly accountable for making a profit shall be involved in creating and distributing knowledge that the company can use to make a profit.
- Our philosophy is simple: Every time we do some-

thing, we should try to do it better than the last time.

- No matter where knowledge comes from, the key to reaping a big return is to leverage that knowledge by replicating it throughout the company so that each unit is not learning in isolation and reinventing the wheel.
- We must view relationships as a coming together that allows us to do something no other two parties can do, and that is make the pie bigger, to our mutual advantage.

To illustrate his point, Browne cites the following case:

"We were drilling lots of horizontal wells, and it occurred to us that we didn't know what was going on. Was the entire horizontal well producing? Did we drill too much or too little? There was no available device that could tell us, which was surprising, because the whole industry was drilling horizontal wells. So we went to Schlumberger, the oil field services company, and said, 'We have one or two rudimentary ideas on how to do this, so we'd like to get together with you. We need the tool, and this could be a wonderful business opportunity for you. As a way to·share the development costs, we'll kick in some of the cash, and volunteer some of our wells to test the tool.'

"We pooled our intellectual and financial resources and Schlumberger built a prototype tool, which looked like a piece of pipe you put down wells. We asked Schlumberger to make it available to us before offering it to everyone in the world. The result was that we got a tool that has taught us a lot about making horizontal wells even more effective, and Schlumberger got a new business" (Browne and Prokesch 1997).

Thinking, planning, strategizing, innovating, learning. All these steps are essential to competing successfully in the global arena. Given the rapid change that is sweeping through every aspect of business, these actions prompt all of us to rethink the way we do things. Simple things. Complex things. The routine and the exceptional. This is critically important because once-reliable guides for managerial action— call them the rules of business—no longer exist. This fundamental change has evolved with little or no advance warning. Flying under the radar of corporate policies and business school textbooks, it has brought a daunting new reality to the challenge of growing and managing businesses.

Case in point: The rules once provided that companies could evolve their product lines over gentle, rhythmic patterns of time. In this environment, the development of new models could be guided by the flow of the calendar. For decades, automakers could synchronize their watches, jointly announcing the availability of new-model Fords, Chryslers, and Chevrolets in the same autumn selling season. There was order to the system. No longer. Today, the rush to attack and acquire market share is so fierce and unrelenting that innovations provide but a fleeting advantage that will often erode within months instead of years. The Silicon Valley slogan "Eat lunch and you are lunch" is more than a reflection of the increasingly intense American work ethic. It demonstrates that in an environment virtually bereft of the old rules of conducting business there is no safety net. Every process, procedure, rule of thumb, and standard ratio is being challenged, reengineered, and morphed into a new form.

Iconoclasm and creativity are now the keys to success. For generations companies built moats between themselves and their competitors. Today the most successful companies build bridges. And that's only the beginning. Increasingly, managers must adopt, execute, and orchestrate what appear to be conflicting policies. Embrace competitors while simultaneously joint-venturing with them. On one hand, it is schizophrenic, on the other, it is essential. More and more, those who can examine the code, challenge it, and rewrite it for success in their companies, fields, and industries will be the leaders and role models. This part intellectual/part pragmatic process is a way of thinking and acting that is central to the Extreme Management philosophy and methodology espoused at AMP.

All of the lessons and exercises revealed in this chapter can help you to seize advantage, build profit margins, and respond positively to change. But remember that while these competitive strategies and tactics are focused on increasing your market share at the expense of your competition, to retain the business you acquire, you will need to add another crucial element (to be explored in the following chapter) to your arsenal of weapons: world-class customer service.

4

THE DISCIPLINE OF
SWAT TEAM SERVICE

Every business manager in every market has to answer a common question: How do I achieve a high-quality standard in every aspect of my team or organization? All too often, the response is a cliché that gives nothing but lip service to the issue. That's because to many, quality is a soft issue that fails to merit the intellectual input or strategic direction of finance, marketing, or technology. Although few will admit it, this all too common view of quality is superficial and simplistic: Put quality standards in place and assign people to make sure they're observed.

Fortunately, others who recognize the critical importance of achieving superior quality are more reflective and creative in the way they approach it. They are determined to understand the fundamental components and dynamics of quality service and to re-

arrange the pieces so that the process achieves un-
paralleled results. Often this involves challenging the
standard assumptions and practices and replacing
them with new ways of doing things.

Some years ago, the CEO of a global consulting company was telling me how important it was for his firm
to deliver flawless services to its clients. In the course
of a long and impassioned monologue, he referred to
the fact that his company had established an intricate
web of departments, rules, procedures, and direc-
tives—all designed to ensure that the highest level of
customer service was achieved and sustained. But instead of patting himself on the back and citing this as
evidence that the firm had the service challenge licked,
he revealed a deep-seated concern based on skepti-
cism that the system—no matter how intricate and
well conceived—could do it all. He proceeded to reveal this concern in an interesting analogy.

"I've been buying M&M candies for more than forty
years," he said. "It's a childhood addiction that has
never abated. Through the years, I've probably bought
more than five thousand bags of M&M's. And you know
something, I've never had a bad one. Not one bag that
was spoiled or stale or crushed or discolored. You can
attribute this to great quality controls, but I've been
managing businesses long enough to know that it takes
more than that: The Mars family has made quality a
cornerstone of their company. It is woven into everything management and employees do. It is a standard,
a religion, and a force that over time has become second nature.

"Any company that wants to achieve a best-of-breed
level of quality has to recognize the importance of
this extra dimension. Without it, all the standards and

procedures and mission statements will come to naught. They'll prove to be rules that were meant to be broken."

The Discipline of SWAT Team Service offers a mix of new ideas and fresh perspectives on the best methods to make superior service second nature in an organization. Some may be familiar while others will be introduced to you for the first time. But in all cases, this section provides approaches that can help make the crucial transition from total quality mission statements to pragmatic quality programs that deliver what they promise. AMP professors and the students who have analyzed, prescribed, and implemented quality-raising methodologies in the challenging crucible of the marketplace help to show the process in a new light, in order to better understand its dynamics and to find innovative ways of putting it to work.

The Ultimate Synergy: Leveraging the Service-Profit Chain

AMP brings the issue of delivering quality service to the top of the needs hierarchy by demonstrating that one can draw a straight line between superior service and long-term profit growth. And true to their approach, it does so by providing an epiphany on this correlation and demonstrating how it can be leveraged.

The program emphasizes the importance of people—both customers and employees—and how linking them can leverage performance through a powerful phenomenon known as the service-profit chain (Heskett et al. 1994).

"Customer loyalty is a major contributor to long-term profit growth—and to win customer loyalty, the business must first satisfy the customer repeatedly," says professor Earl Sasser. "The service-profit chain is an equation that establishes the relationship between employee satisfaction, customer loyalty, and profitability."

The links in the chain are as follows:

- Profit and growth are stimulated primarily by customer loyalty.
- Loyalty is a direct result of customer satisfaction.
- Satisfaction is largely influenced by the value of services provided to customers.
- Value is created by satisfied, loyal, and productive employees.
- Employee satisfaction, in turn, results primarily from high-quality support services and policies that enable employees to serve customers well.

Customer satisfaction—a critical component of maximum profitability—delivers four valuable benefits:

1. Customers stay with the company longer.
2. Customers deepen their relationship with the company.
3. Customers demonstrate less price sensitivity.
4. Customers care enough about the company to recommend its products or services to others.

In the ideal situation a seamless integration links all the critical dynamics of top customer service. The company guides, nurtures, and empowers its employees, and the employees play a vital role in securing customer satisfaction and the benefits that accrue from it.

When companies are effective in satisfying their employees, employees stay longer, make a deeper commitment to the business, recommend ways to improve the company's products and services, and work harder to satisfy the customer.

An interview with Professor Len Schlesinger, a former Harvard Business School faculty member, now senior vice president, counselor to the president, and professor of sociology and public policy, Brown University, and an expert on the importance of customer service—and how it is delivered by the most successful companies:

Q. Many companies fail to leverage the service-profit chain. What are the major obstacles to doing so?

A. The most common obstacle is that companies view the lifetime value of a customer relationship as the arithmetic sum of the transactions it conducts with that person. This kind of tunnel vision means they don't really seek to build relationships. Instead, they focus solely on conducting transactions or sales one by one. This is shortsighted because it diminishes the synergies that come into play when enduring relationships are built and nurtured. For example, they forfeit the opportunities for cross-selling, generating word of mouth, gaining referrals, and building barriers to competitive encroachment.

Carl Sewell, co-author of *Customers for Life,* expressed this concept so well. He made us see that consummating transactions—in his case, selling cars—was important but not as important as unleashing the power of the service-profit chain. Rather than squeezing every customer for top dollar per vehicle, Sewell was willing to be flexible on price in order to capture the customer relationship. And once he had that relationship, he serviced the customer relentlessly. This delivered an advantage many businesspeople are blind to: Through the power of word of mouth, he expanded the customer from an individual to a group of people the individual influenced—including neighbors, employees, relatives, and friends. Equally important, by adopting a holistic approach to customer relationships—as opposed to a transactional focus (sell the metal, sell the metal), he maintained customer relationships for years and sold these people automobile maintenance, accessories, financing, and so on.

Creating a financial system that truly captures the financial dynamics of customer relationships is important. Unless managers can assign true value to all the components of customer relationships, they are stuck with a mass of idiosyncratic information that makes it difficult if not impossible to understand where the money really is, and how to attract it.

Q. There are a lot of smart managers out there. Why don't they see the financial advantages of moving from a focus on transactions to a focus on relationships?

A. In many cases, it's because they don't want to.

Their cultural bias is so skewed to rewarding people on a transactional basis that they are reluctant to change their internal model to one that rewards people for building and maintaining relationships. Related to this, they often make the mistake of thinking they own the customer relationship. In the 1970s and 1980s, the banks said, "The branch system is too expensive. By moving people to ATMs and PCs, we can save as much as $500 per customer per year. In effect, we'll bypass the branches and move customers to transact directly with headquarters." I remember seeing charts that showed:

COST PER CUSTOMER	
BRANCH SYSTEM	$500
ATM	$25
PC	$10

Based on this projected business model, the bankers said, "We'll go from $500 per customer to $10." But like many businesses, they have learned that neither the branch nor the corporate headquarters owns the relationship. The customer owns the relationship. And the customers decided they wanted more than a series of efficient transactions: They wanted service, measured in part by their ability to select the type of banking they wanted, when they wanted it. That means the same customer will—at various times—want to visit a branch, use an ATM, or bank by phone. In order to maintain relationships and remain competitive, the banks have had to offer all three banking options, at a cost of not $10, but $535. Yet still, profits at the best banks have risen.

This case illustrates the value customers place on relationships. It also sends a message to businesspeople determined to grow their companies: Look beyond the arithmetic value of individual transactions to all the ways you can serve a customer. Your performance will improve as you leverage the service-profit chain.

Fred Smith, the founder and CEO of Federal Express, puts it this way: It's People, Service, Profit, not Profit, Service, People.

In Poorly Managed Companies, People Are Problems . . . In Well-Managed Companies, People Are Problem-Solvers

Customers expect rapid response when mistakes are made or there are lapses in service. This leads us to a hallmark of high-caliber service organizations: Front-line employees are important not only for delivering the products, but are instrumental in addressing and correcting post-sale problems and related issues. At that time the primary goal is to seek out and eliminate such bugs in the future.

But rapid response and attentive follow-through are only possible when people are empowered to make decisions and are motivated to solve problems. Creating a work environment that encourages this is key to leveraging the power of the service-profit chain.

Scott Cook, executive committee chairman of Intuit, details his company's philosophy when it comes to such matters:

"We want to occupy all of the mental capabilities of our employees. If they are just doing their jobs, we only have part of what they can contribute to the company and our customers. By encouraging them to go beyond the literal boundaries of their jobs—to make suggestions for improvement—we gain the full potential of their contributions to the business."

Intuit has fashioned a workforce of customer service fanatics. To accomplish this, Cook has instituted the following measures designed to produce empowered and motivated employees who are committed to ever higher standards of customer service and satisfaction.

• Identify customers' true needs. In the process of researching market potential for Quicken, the company's personal finance software, Cook discovered that more than anything else the product would have to help consumers deal with the drudgery of balancing their checkbooks. Minus this fundamental feature, Quicken could not build a significant beachhead in the marketplace. Driving this point home to his staff, Cook found a way to make it simple and clear. Holding a pen in the air, he would declare: This is the competition. Unless we can create a product that is faster and more accurate than this, we will fail.

- Design products that are easy to use. Instead of seeking complex solutions that satisfied software engineers, Cook instructed his people to focus on the simplicity and compelling qualities of computer games. They placed primary focus on the voice of the customer.

Intuit reversed the traditional corporate hierarchy. Instead of relegating customer service to the lowest end of the power structure:

> Traditional Model:
> Software Engineering
> Marketing
> Customer Service

Cook placed customer service at the top:

> Intuit Model:
> Customer Service
> Software Engineering
> Marketing

This organizational structure is based on the conviction that customer service people learn more about product strengths and weaknesses than anyone else in the company, and that properly empowered and motivated, they will provide this input to leverage the service-profit chain. In this regard, Intuit provides for customer input to be heard throughout the organization. In most companies, the customer's voice fails to reach key decision-makers or does so in a staggered fashion. But in the well-run service organization, such as Intuit, the customer's voice is heard simultaneously by all key functions and departments.

Intuit's Relentless, Out-of-the-Box Customer Service Passion

To make customer service an essential part of its culture, Intuit teaches employees to go beyond the veneer of superficial concern, making the customer's voice omnipresent throughout the company. The following are examples of customer focus, Intuit style:

- At company meetings, management demonstrates Intuit's order of priorities by addressing customer service trends, problems, and victories before getting around to the traditional headliners of revenues and profits. This sends the Intuit message that customer service comes before all else.
- Thank-you letters are posted on the company's walls. When customers write to crow about the added value they receive from Intuit employees, their letters are treated as big news. (Compare this to the traditional response of filing away customer compliments in a desk drawer.)
- Intuit staffers representing all departments and functions perform monthly service manning the customer service telephones. Sitting in the hot seat—empowered to listen and respond—they gain a real-world view of the issues that can damage the company's franchise, and how to address them decisively. Getting behind the wheel in this manner

takes customer service out of the abstract, and turns it into something concrete.

An interview with Professor Earl Sasser:

Q. How do you define loyal customers?

A. Loyal customers account for an unusually high proportion of the sales and profit growth of successful service providers. In some organizations, loyalty is measured in terms of whether or not a customer is on the company rolls. But several companies have found that their most loyal customers—the top 20 percent of total customers—not only provide all the profits but also cover losses incurred in dealing with less loyal customers.

Because of the link between loyal customers and profit, Banc One measures depth of relationship—the number of available related financial services, such as checking, lending, and safe deposit boxes, actually used by customers. Recognizing the same relationship, Taco Bell measures "share of stomach" to assess the company's sales against all other food purchases a customer can potentially make. As a result, the fast food chain is trying to reach consumers through kiosks, carts, trucks, and the shelves of supermarkets.

Q. Do measurements of customer profitability include profits from referrals?

A. Companies that measure the stream of revenue and profits from loyal customers (retention) and repeat sales often overlook referrals. For example, Intuit provides high-quality, free lifetime service for a personal finance software package that sells for a relatively modest sum. The strategy makes sense when the value of a loyal customer is considered—a revenue stream of several thousands of dollars from software updates, supplies, and new customer referrals.

Q. Why do customers defect?

A. It's important to find out not only where defectors go, but also why they defect. Was it because of poor service, price, or value? Answers to these questions provide information about whether or not existing strategies are working. In addition, exit interviews of customers can have real sales impact. For example, at one credit card service organization, a phone call to question cardholders that had stopped using their cards led to the immediate reinstatement of one third of the defectors.

Q. Is customer satisfaction data gathered in an objective and consistent fashion?

A. The weakest measurements being used by the companies we have studied concern customer satisfaction. At some companies, high levels of reported customer satisfaction are contradicted by continuing declines in sales and profits. Upon closer observation, we discovered that the service providers were "gaming" the data, using manipulative methods for collecting customer satisfaction data. In one extreme case, an automobile dealer sent a questionnaire to recent buyers with the highest marks already filled in, requiring owners to alter the marks only if they disagreed. Companies can, however, obtain objective results by using third party interviews; mystery shopping by unidentified, paid observers; or technological methods, like touch-screen television.

Q. How is information concerning customers' perceptions of value shared with those responsible for designing a product or service?

A. Relaying information concerning customer expectations to those responsible for design often requires the formation of teams of people responsible for sales, operations, service, or product design, as well as the frequent assignment of service designers to tasks requiring field contact with customers. Intuit has created this kind of capability in product development teams. And all Intuit employees, including the CEO, must periodically work on the customer service phones. Similarly, at Southwest, those responsible for flight scheduling periodically work shifts in the company's terminals to get a feel for the impact of schedules on customer and employee satisfaction.

How to Turn Angry Customers into Loyal Patrons

Let's explore the service issue from another perspective: From time to time it's inevitable that you will anger customers and jeopardize goodwill. But you can turn that problem into an opportunity to build an even stronger position with the customer.

This is known as managing the art and science of service recovery. According to Harvard professors Earl

Sasser and James Heskett, as well as Christopher Hart, president of the Cambridge, Massachusetts-based TQM Group, a good recovery can turn angry, frustrated customers into loyal ones. It can, in fact, create more goodwill than if things had gone smoothly in the first place.

A Harvard Business School case study demonstrates how Club Med–Cancún, part of the Paris-based Club Méditerranée, recovered from a service nightmare and won the loyalty of one group of vacationers.

The vacationers had nothing but trouble getting from New York to their Mexican destination. The flight took off six hours late, made two unexpected stops, and circled for thirty minutes before landing. Because of all of the delays and mishaps, the plane was en route for ten hours longer than planned and ran out of food and drinks. It finally arrived at two o'clock in the morning, with a landing so rough that oxygen masks and luggage dropped from overhead. By the time the plane pulled up to the gate, the soured passengers were faint with hunger and convinced that their vacation was ruined before it had even started. One lawyer on board was already collecting names and addresses for a class action suit.

The general manager of the Cancún resort and a legend throughout the organization for his ability to satisfy customers, got word of the horrendous flight and immediately created an antidote. He took half the staff to the airport, where they laid out a table of snacks and drinks and set up a stereo system to play lively music. As the guests filed through the gate, they received personal greetings, help with their bags, a sympathetic ear, and a chauffeured ride to the resort. Waiting for them at Club Med was a lavish banquet, complete with mariachi band and champagne. Moreover, the staff had rallied other guests to wait up and greet the newcomers, and the partying continued until sunrise. Many guests said it was the most fun they'd had since college.

In the end the vacationers had a better experience than if their flight from New York had gone like clockwork. Although the company probably couldn't measure it, Club Méditerranée won market share that night. After all, the battle for market share is won not by analyzing demographic trends, rating points, and other global measures but rather by pleasing customers one at a time.

Sometimes creative companies take the offensive by going out of their way to address a customer problem for which they share no blame—all with the goal of initiating a powerful new relationship. Consider this anecdote from the recipient of such unexpected exceptional service.

"A while back, there was a very bad fire in my house," the individual recounts. "The next day, I was raking through my possessions, my family sitting on the front stoop, when a Domino's Pizza truck pulled up. The driver got out and approached us with two pizzas. I told him I didn't order any pizza and explained that our house had just burned. 'I know,' he replied. 'I saw you when I drove by half an hour ago. I figured you must be really hungry, so my store manager and I decided to make a couple of pizzas for you. We put everything on them. If that's not how you like them, I'll take them back and get them made the way you like—on the house.' I couldn't believe it. Now, do you think I'd ever buy pizza from anyone else?"

Another case of service recovery involves Stew

Leonard's, a retail dairy store in Norwalk, Connecticut, renowned for its service. One evening at about 6:00 P.M., Stew Leonard, Jr., found a crisply worded complaint written by a customer from just a half an hour earlier: "I made a special stop on my way home from work to buy chicken breasts for dinner, but you're sold out. Now I'll have to eat a TV dinner instead." As Leonard was reading the complaint, a Perdue chicken truck happened to pull up to the store's loading dock. Within minutes, someone was heading off to the frustrated customer's house with a complimentary two-pound package of fresh chicken breasts.

Remember you are bound to make mistakes in business, but those mistakes don't have to cost you precious customer relationships. Inevitable lapses in service might jeopardize customer relationships, but that's not to say that these lapses will invariably sever those relationships.

If you respond rapidly and creatively to address a precarious customer service situation, you can often stabilize that relationship and turn the individual who might have become your worst enemy into your best— and hopefully most profitable—friend.

THE PARADOX OF THE SATISFIED CUSTOMER

Managing customer service can be a complex and dynamic challenge rife with hidden traps. In many cases, a satisfied customer is actually a time bomb in disguise. Studies indicate that in highly competitive markets there is a wide gulf between satisfied and completely satisfied customers. And the former is far more likely to switch to another supplier. Primary Research Corporation's study of retail banking customers found the completely satisfied customers were approximately 72 percent more likely to be loyal than satisfied customers.

Professor Earl Sasser and Thomas O. Jones (president of Elm Square Technologies) view the paradox of the satisfied customer this way:

What is the overarching lesson? That customers are reasonable, but they want to be completely satisfied. If they are not and have a choice, they can be easily lured away by the competition.

In today's turbulent world, measuring customers' outward loyalty does not suffice. Nor does knowing whether the satisfaction-loyalty relationship a company enjoys with the majority of its customers is the norm for this market. It is essential to understand what portion of customers' seeming loyalty is true loyalty based on a company's delivery of superior value and what part is artificial. Measuring customer satisfaction is one of the safest ways to obtain this information.

Most managers should be concerned rather than heartened if the majority of their customers fall into the satisfied category. Those customers have reasons for not being completely satisfied. Some element of their experience with the company is not acceptable, and that shortfall in performance is sufficient for them to consider alternatives. Some might ask: Why did these customers say they were satisfied in the first place? The answer is: Regardless of how they feel, customers of companies with a reasonably good product or service quality tend to find it difficult to respond negatively to customer satisfaction surveys. As a result, their satisfaction responses typically fall in the upper end of the scale—a 4 or 5 on a scale of 1 to 5.

Rather than thinking of customers as loyal or disloyal, managers would be better off treating them as three separate groups:

INTERPRETING LEVELS OF SATISFACTION		
RESPONSE	DESCRIPTION	LOYALTY
5	Completely satisfied	Very loyal
3–4	Satisfied	Easily switched to a competitor
1–2	Dissatisfied	Very disloyal

An interview with a private investor and AMP graduate on business-to-business customer relations:

Q. Many companies say they are committed to forging partnerships with their b to b customers but, in most cases, it's just lip service. How can managers actually walk the walk?

A. By fundamentally changing your view of the customer relationship. Instead of seeing the customer as a businessperson for whom you provide products and services, start to think of yourself and the customer as two people bound by a shared fate. If you make the customer's job easier, if you make the customer perform better, if you make the customer look better, the customer wins and so do you. To get to this perspective, and make it work day in and day out, you have to see yourself as the customer. Engage in a visioning exercise that allows you to get into their heads, identify their goals, and learn the pressures they face. Interview them about this. Talk to their customers and suppliers. Understand who they have to please—what happens if they do and what befalls them if they don't. This will sensitize you in a way that helps you identify what you have to deliver, and how you have to deliver it, to keep the customer happy and the relationship strong.

Q. This sounds as if you really have to get close to the person and work as one. In that case, what happens if you don't like the customer? If the chemistry is bad?

A. Chemistry should have nothing to do with it. The fact is, you will do all of the above for the people you like and feel close to because you have an emotional desire to help them succeed. The real trick is to apply that same understanding and sensitivity to all customers. Once you begin to take this approach, it becomes part of your corporate culture. And it turns into a highly effective competitive advantage. Wouldn't you rather buy from people who take your interests to heart?

As we have discovered, powerful and often invisible dynamics in every aspect of a company's culture, organization, leadership, and customer relationships take a toll on a business by impacting its competitive position and, ultimately, its financial performance. We say these dynamics are often invisible in part because many experienced managers are unable to read the early warning signs that appear in the hieroglyphics of business: financial reports, balance sheets, and poll data. Shoring up this weak link in managerial capabilities through innovative ways or looking at the financial picture is an important component of Advanced Management Program training that we will explore in the following chapter.

5

UNLOCKING THE BLACK BOX
OF FINANCE

Effective managers are inquisitive, informed, skeptical, and determined to have all the facts at hand before making a decision. But this model often breaks down when financial components are central to the decision-making process. Because they are not secure in their ability to challenge the numbers presented by the financial people—or to challenge the thinking behind the numbers—they will often make decisions without being fully informed.

In business, this managerial blind spot reflects the fact that most companies are informally divided into two camps:

- The finance people.
- Everyone else.

Typically, the numbers people build their financial models, assumptions, and projections with minimal interference from the operations side of the business. Likewise, line managers often disregard the financial models and projections they don't grasp. This produces a dangerous dichotomy that leads to poor and often misleading decision making.

"AMP makes it clear that you are in a much stronger position if you understand the dynamics of finance," says AMP graduate Dr. Kenneth Rosen of Sikorsky Aircraft. "It's not merely for the sake of understanding another discipline, but in order to make sounder decisions likely to produce a greater return for your department, business unit, or company. Before my AMP experience, if a finance person told me that the internal rate of return on a proposed project was 15 percent, I had to accept that assumption at face value. But what if it was wrong? What if it was based on bad numbers or illogical thinking? Because I lacked the skills to challenge the assumption, I had little choice but to accept it. No more. Now when a finance person presents me with internal rate of return assumptions on a proposed project, I have the knowledge to challenge those assumptions. I find that when I do so, the finance person and I often arrive at a deeper truth. What's more, decisions I make based on this complete picture are likely to produce better results for my department, and for the company."

From its earliest days, AMP's central mission—and its greatest value to those who are exposed to the totality of its learning experience—is to groom exceptional managers. Unlike the vast majority of businesspeople—even highly ranked executives who rest comfortably within functional silos—AMP grads are taught to stretch themselves and expand their perspectives well beyond their personal comfort zones.

Unlocking the black box of finance is one way of working toward this goal.

Mastering the DuPont Formula and Other Tricks for Decoding Financial Statements

Numbers are the universal language of finance, the raw materials of balance sheets and P&L statements. To the untutored they appear to be little more than a parade of digits on a computer printout. But managers seeking to lead business units must learn to read between, above, and around the numbers to uncover two key indicators: proportion and direction. This begins with a change of perspective.

"The time has come to stop viewing finance as a black box only the company's numbers people can crack," says retired AMP professor emeritus Robert H. Hayes. "To make this intellectual transition, you have to learn to look beyond the complexities of corporate accounting and finance to the broader conceptual truths and trends the numbers communicate. When you can do that, it's like you're wearing glasses fitted with financial lenses. One look through these lenses and the managers we teach say: 'Oh my God, that's great. I can see!'"

This brings us to the concepts of proportion and direction. Think of these principles as numbers-driven status reports on the corporation's fiscal well-being. Here's a crash course on deciphering them.

Proportion

Your company's financial reports reveal interesting and important information on the proportion of physical assets (plant and equipment) versus cash flow. This is important because the speed at which a company turns over its assets reveals how capital-intensive that business is. If the company turns over assets only one time a year, management needs to recognize that it must earn a substantial profit margin per sale. For example, assume your company sells sandwiches. If you sell fourteen sandwiches an hour, you turn over assets quickly, and can afford low margins per sale. But if you sell only a single sandwich a day, you must earn a steep margin per sale. The key point is that if you turn over assets slowly, and earn little profit per sale, you will not be adequately profitable.

It's the proportion of cash flow versus physical assets on the balance sheet that tells you how hard you have to work those physical assets to make an adequate profit. The larger the investment in assets one has to make in a business in relation to sales, the greater the margin one needs to make on each sale.

With this in mind, the DuPont Formula is revealing. Developed by the DuPont Company, and widely imitated by companies in many industries, the formula holds that profit over sales, sales over assets, and assets over shareholder equity equals return on equity:

$$\frac{\text{Profit}}{\text{Sales}} \times \frac{\text{Sales}}{\text{Assets}} \times \frac{\text{Assets}}{\text{Shareholder Equity}} = \text{Return on Equity}$$

An interesting aspect of proportion revealed from the DuPont Formula sheds light on a key component of the company's net worth—the assets the business owns and who paid for them. This is articulated by the third component of the DuPont Formula (assets over shareholder equity). A company with considerable assets but relatively little equity has been financed mostly with other people's money, and thus is highly leveraged.

When you look at assets and liabilities, what you are really seeing is:

> Liabilities: who paid for the assets
> Assets: what the money bought

This aspect of proportion is important because it reveals the extent of the company's leverage.

Direction

A general sense of a company's direction can be gleaned from its financial statements. Sometimes relationships between a company's resources and its sales growth get out of whack. If a company must invest a disproportionate amount of assets for each dollar of sales increase, then the company will be pouring extra money into its assets to such an extent that it will eventually exhaust its financial backer's desire to lend and eventually it will run out of money.

For example, to grow by 20 percent on a sustainable basis, management must continue to add 20 percent to the retained earnings. This is reflected in the balance sheet in shareholder equity. If shareholder equity grows by only 10 percent annually, the company can grow by only 10 percent at a sustainable level. In this scenario the only way to exceed 10 percent growth is to increase profitability or acquire additional debt— the latter option subjecting the company to greater leverage. In this way, a balance sheet provides a snapshot of the company's direction, how it can be maintained, and where it may veer off course. Thus, we begin to see the power of looking at the gestalt of the numbers to identify proportion and direction.

EXPLORING THE APPLE TREE ANALOGY

As companies take on debt, they have to understand that the more debt they assume the further out on the leverage limb they go. Think of it as climbing out on the thinning bough of an apple tree in order to reach the biggest fruit. Why do companies take this risk? Because borrowing money provides greater options than if they use their own capital.

"The more you squeeze down the value of shareholder equity to the size of the assets you are financing, the higher the return on equity you can get," says Professor Robert Hayes. "So as you go out on that debt limb, you may want to keep going because even though it gets shakier and shakier, the apples get bigger and bigger, as measured by return on equity. Put simply, you are generating greater and greater returns with less shareholder equity.

"Once you learn to read balance sheets, you discover that the numbers can make companies look deceptively profitable. Consider the company that declares they earned 100 percent on shareholder equity. Sounds impressive, but the financials reveal that the company didn't really do well in profit or asset utilization. Management can report a fantastic return on equity because there is virtually no shareholder equity financing the business. It is fueled almost exclusively on debt.

"This put the company out on the proverbial limb. Why? Because the company's profitability may not be sustainable. In order to grow and maintain its profits, the company must keep borrowing money, but sooner or later the supply of capital available to the company will be exhausted.

"Think of this insight as a snapshot of the company's direction. The financials provide more than numbers. They can tell us where the company is headed. This is why I tell AMP participants to climb into a virtual helicopter and view financial information from a vantage point high above the trees. Whenever possible, avoid getting bogged down in detailed financial analysis. This takes you out of the helicopter and into the trees, where you may miss the big issues that should be factored into management decision making. When you face a problem where you have to understand the anatomy of the problem in order to solve it and it has financial overtones, the first thing to do is to get an overall sense of the anatomy from the financial point of view. You can always swoop down later to attack a specific issue. But don't lose sight of the whole."

An interesting example of the DuPont Formula involves an interesting case taught at the Harvard Business School, that of the Clarkson Lumber Company.

"Clarkson stocked lumber, door frames, sashes, and the like for sale to contractors. Things were going very well for Clarkson; he had a significant base of customers, was increasing his sales, and was making a profit. But there was a problem: As Clarkson grew his company, he found the need to borrow more and more money—way beyond what he expected. His profit (the return that he earned on the portion of his capital that was his own money, as opposed to what he had borrowed) looked great, but he was getting further and further out on the debt limb."

The case reveals that Clarkson was making a good return on his ownership funds, as expressed by the return on investment. Remember, Professor Hayes teaches that the DuPont Formula looks at the profitability that is being earned on the owner's money. That's the basic calculation it does, and then it explains it. It pulls apart that summary calculation. Assume that Mr. Clarkson is making 25 percent a year on his money. That's a very good return. But it's important to understand why he is doing extremely well.

In order to understand that, Professor Hayes tells his AMP students to separate the calculation into three components that contribute to the return that's being earned on the owner's money:

The first component is the margin that you can make on every dollar that you sell. In Clarkson's case, it's a very small margin. He's a middleman. He buys his inventory of construction materials from a larger distributor and then sells pieces to the contractors. He makes a very small margin on each sale.

The second part of this formula concerns how efficiently he uses the assets he needs to run the business. If we think about this in terms of the balance sheet, the assets are on one side, and the sources of funds are on the other. So, in this case, we have Clarkson's major assets—inventory, a truck, office furniture (we'll assume he rents his office), and the credit he extends to his customers (accounts receivable). The question is how efficiently is Clarkson using his assets? How many times a year is he turning the assets over? Let's say that Clarkson's assets total $100,000 and his sales for the year totaled $300,000. That means he's getting a turnover on his assets of three times annually.

That's the second part of the DuPont Formula as Professor Hayes teaches it. To recap, the first part details what he makes on every dollar he sells—in Clarkson's case, a thin margin. The second part details how many dollars he sells compared to the assets he must invest to generate his sales and maintain his business.

The third component of the DuPont Formula—this is the critical one for Mr. Clarkson—is how much money he has invested and how much money banks and others have invested in his company.

Imagine Clarkson has $100,000 worth of assets. Because of double entry bookkeeping there must be $100,000 on the other side of the balance sheet, which consists of liabilities from those who have lent him money, plus his own investment in the business.

So in the case of Clarkson Lumber, there is $100,000 in assets and $100,000 on the other side of the balance sheet that reveals who paid for the assets. Clarkson is making a very good return on his owner's investment because it is so small—let's say $20,000. Seeing as he's mostly using other people's money, he gets a very thin margin from his business every time he makes a sale.

Professor Hayes likes to illustrate this concept to his AMP students in terms of slices of bologna—you get a very thin slice of bologna if you're only a middleman and you only take a small margin, as does Mr. Clarkson. Well, in order to make a decent sandwich, you have to have a lot of slices.

In this specific case, Mr. Clarkson is putting up $20,000, with the rest of his $100,000 worth of assets paid for with other people's money. So although Clarkson gets a very small amount of profit on each sales dollar, and may only be turning over his assets three times a year when it should be five or six, since he only invested $20,000 it looks like he's doing just great. But the fact is, in order to grow the business, Clarkson is going to have to invest more assets. To accomplish this, Clarkson's asset base must grow to $200,000.

Again, double entry bookkeeping says that the other side of the balance sheet must also show $200,000 (composed of the liabilities of people who have lent Clarkson money in one form or another in addition to his own investment). But where is Clarkson's money coming from? It's not coming from profit, because Clarkson's not making that much profit. So, the only way to make the two sides balance is to push further out on the debt limb, to borrow more and more money relative to Clarkson's own investment. This is like the difference between a person who owns a house with 25 percent owner equity versus 75 percent borrowed, compared to a house where only 5 percent is owned by the owner and 95 percent is owned by the banks. That second scenario is the direction Mr. Clarkson is heading.

Assuming the company continues to grow, how much additional assets will Clarkson need and who will pay for those assets? As you engage in these what-if scenarios, and you explore the consequences of getting larger and larger, you reach a fundamental truth.

If Clarkson can't make his slices of bologna thicker, and if he can't turn over his assets any more frequently (so he doesn't have to have as many of them), the only way he can grow is to get the banks to lend him more money.

This brings us to the essential point of the DuPont Formula as Professor Hayes explains it to AMP students:

Here is an entrepreneur who is showing a great return on his modest amount of equity in the business. He owns only a small percentage of the company, so any modest increase in the value of the company is going to make the return on his ownership look fantastic. But the fact is that this is often a formula for disaster. You can't keep doing that. Unless you can demonstrate a longer-term perspective, the banks will stop lending to you. Case closed.

When It Comes to Global Currency Hedging, the One Sure Way to Lose Money May Be to Insure Against It

Perhaps you already confront the complexities of making decisions with global issues and repercussions in mind. If not, maybe someday you will. Either way, you're sure to find the challenge of international finance particularly nettlesome. Consider, for example, the unpredictability of global currency fluctuations and the impact this can have as you seek to convert overseas earnings into dollars. Caught in the shifting sands of multinational finance, profits can quickly turn to losses.

"No problem," managers often say. "We'll simply engage in hedging techniques designed to eliminate the risk." The problem is, it's not that simple.

Hedging currency is really a kind of insurance policy that can diminish or control risk, but like all forms of insurance, it carries a price tag. When you look closely at the levels and dynamics of currency fluctuations, the cost of the hedging insurance is often tantamount to throwing away money. That's because currencies don't move in one direction for protracted periods of time. When the dollar rises against the yen, for example, you have to retain a long-term perspective, recognizing that, in time, the disparity will narrow or reverse, with the yen rising against the dollar. Because a global company's gains and losses are bound to be a wash over time, why allow profits to erode through the cost of hedging? In many cases, the only justifiable reason is to manage shareholders' expectations. When this appearance factor is not a critical objective, it may be sounder—from a long-term earnings viewpoint—to eschew hedging and accept the market's tendency to achieve equilibrium.

One way of looking at hedging is as a game that tries to create cosmetically stable operating results for a group of investors. Professor Hayes suggests that these investors, if they were more sophisticated, would say, "Don't waste money on this kind of thing, because over the long term, it's all going to wash out."

Of course, even the savviest managers must often make decisions in which political considerations outweigh financial concerns.

"As a member of Tiffany's board of directors, I faced

this issue head-on as the company debated the pros and cons of currency hedging," Hayes recalls. "In presenting the side of the issue that often goes unstated, I said: 'We may be making money on our hedging strategy when the currency market is moving in an unfavorable direction. But because we are presumably going to engage in this hedging strategy on an ongoing basis, when the currencies are moving in our favor we'll be spending money for no good reason and our earnings per share will be penalized.'

"Why should we provide that kind of hand-holding to investors when there is no economic payoff over the long term? When everything washes out, we will have spent millions of dollars on insurance policies that fail to provide net economic gain. That much said, we did have a valid need to provide comfort to the shareholders. So the board—myself included—voted to hedge. The important thing is that we did so with full knowledge of the issues and options. Equally important, this knowledge arms us with the flexibility to change our approach over time."

IN BUSINESS, THE BEST TIME TO PERFORM AN AUTOPSY IS WHEN THE PATIENT IS STILL ALIVE

You've been named to a new managerial position. Congratulations! Now the question is, what will you do to put your stamp on the business unit? Surprisingly, the best approach is to kill it! Or at least to pretend that it is dead and immediately proceed to conduct a financial autopsy.

Reluctant as they may be to admit it, newly appointed managers don't really know how the organizations they have inherited make money, or, in spite of the published numbers, if they really make money at all. That's because these new managers:

- Don't fully understand the unique dynamics that drive the organization's business model.
- Don't completely accept their predecessor's financial reporting and/or projections which, individually and collectively, have a pervasive influence on its financial performance.

This is precisely why the financial autopsy can prove invaluable. Think of it as an urgent quest for information that reveals what is truly going on beneath the surface. The process seeks to answer such critical questions as:

- What major growth opportunities are embedded in the company's key lines of business?
- If new product or service lines must be established, what impact will this have on the company's capitalization?
- Does the company have adequate capacity to finance its growth through cash flow or debt sources?
- Do current operations generate sufficient capital to fund diversification? To what extent?

The financial autopsy is particularly important because newly installed managers don't step into a vacuum. In the vast majority of cases, they are replacing a predecessor who—in her own attempt to impress and please superiors—has made a set of projections.

Time and again, these projections are unrealistic because they are based on a flawed strategy management has sold to the board. Rather than moving down the primrose path in pursuit of a plan that can't work, a new manager needs to be armed with the knowledge revealed by a financial autopsy, so she can report back to superiors with a clear-cut message: "Our current strategy is wrong. It won't work."

The next step is to return to the fundamentals, developing a business model that is, at the very least, sufficiently profitable and creates an equilibrium between capital needs and the business unit's ability to generate or secure additional capital.

Without such a model in place, growth halts and the business deteriorates. Thus the caveat AMP drills into its graduates: The best time to perform an autopsy is when the patient is still alive.

CREATING SUCCESSFUL BUSINESS MODELS: IT'S ALL IN THE NUMBERS

In every business, many of the traditional ways of doing things are costly and inefficient. This is because no one has instilled a fresh perspective to challenge the norm and develop a new approach. This is where financial evidence can be helpful. It legitimizes the challenge to tradition needed to penetrate to the highest levels of your organization.

Financial evidence helps answer these vital questions:

- Do the company's processes make sense economically?
- Are there more efficient means of achieving similar or improved results?
- What steps, products, employees, and equipment can be eliminated, producing greater cost savings and profitability?

Questions like these must be continually asked in order to guard against standard operating procedures that could cost a business its profits—and cripple your career.

"AMP's case study approach led me to a clearer understanding of how economics can impact the building of a powerful business model," says the World Bank's Oey Meesook. "Thanks to AMP, I've come to recognize that financial aspects, business concepts, and marketing thrust are often closely intermingled. In fact, the drive to achieve a more profitable business model can create the foundation for a unique marketing approach that differentiates the business and delivers strong results."

Meesook goes on to say that AMP's case study of the structure of the Benihana restaurant chain, based in Tokyo, brought the issue into sharper resolution. "I was taken by founder Rocki Aoki's relentless focus on reducing costs by stripping away what traditional thinkers thought to be indispensable fixtures of a successful restaurant. In the process, Aoki created a uniquely appealing environment."

One of the things Aoki took into account in his

business model was that the number one problem of the U.S. restaurant industry is the shortage of skilled labor. Aoki turned this problem into an opportunity by coming up with Benihana's famed hibachi table arrangement, which eliminates the need for a conventional kitchen. Rocki Aoki describes his unconventional approach to restaurant profitability:

"With the hibachi tables, the only skilled person I need is a chef. So I can give an unusual amount of attentive service and still keep labor costs to 10 percent to 12 percent of gross sales (food and beverage) depending on whether a unit is at full volume. In addition, I was able to turn practically the entire restaurant into productive dining space. Only about 22 percent of the total space of a unit is back of the house, including preparation areas, dry and refrigerated storage, employee dressing rooms, and office space. Normally a restaurant requires 30 percent of its total space as back of the house.

"The other thing I discovered is that food storage and waste contribute significantly to the overhead of the typical restaurant. By reducing the menu to only three simple Middle American entrées—steak, chicken, and shrimp—I have virtually no waste and can cut food costs to between 30 percent and 35 percent of food sales depending on the price of meat."

By thinking out of the box and setting aside traditional assumptions in the restaurant industry, Aoki was able to achieve, in one master stroke, a highly efficient financial model synergized with a strong marketing approach.

"The Benihana case illustrates the power of putting a business under a microscope," says Oey Meesook. "By identifying the key elements of his financial model, Aoki was able to achieve both innovation and cost efficiency. This resulted in his accomplishing the two indispensable requirements for business success— he pleased people and he earned a fair profit."

When you boil it down, the great value of AMP lies in the identification, dissection, and application of business models. Through the integrated mix of lectures, case studies, and study groups, the students come to see in sharp relief that success is based not on great ideas, guts, or instinct alone—but on the ability to create and master business models.

These models link together the key components of corporate success—from financial planning to customer-sharing service strategies, from the art of knowledge to the near science of negotiating—and bundle them in an intellectual and pragmatic package that can be used to achieve sustainable market advantage, growth, and profitability. This integrated approach to the managerial process is what shapes AMP students and provides them with a broad view and the corresponding capabilities to help achieve the status of extremely effective leaders armed to run the show—and to do so with world-class success.

EPILOGUE

For more than a half century, Harvard's Advanced Management Program has been enlightening senior corporate executives representing a wide range of industries, nationalities, corporate and social cultures, and economic and educational backgrounds. Given this diversity, it is surprising how united the graduates are in their view of the program as more than a valuable experience: Often it is ranked as a turning point in their lives, one that prepared them for new levels of personal growth and career success.

The question is, how can a course of study at a major university have such a profound impact on these worldly men and women? In the process of interviewing dozens of AMP graduates, a number of key values rose to the surface:

In the day-to-day regimen of corporate management, most executives are preoccupied with the fundamentals of blocking and tackling. AMP provides the opportunity, and the insights, to look through an educational prism and see things in new ways. As the graduates reenter the corporate environment, this leads to fresh approaches that can provide a competitive advantage for their business units and their personal career development.

Many participants arrive at Harvard believing the window has closed on their ability to experience significant growth. After all, they have already managed units, fought the political battles, learned to adapt and cope, and attended hundreds of seminars, forums, and conferences. What more could they really learn, other than purely technical knowledge? Could they really find new and inventive ways of thinking, from the routine to the strategic? From the simple to the sublime? After this experience, virtually all answer with a resounding yes.

In the conversations I conducted one philosophy prevails. It is built into the foundations of the program and the curriculum, as well as the thinking of the men and women who participate in it. All are intelligent, successful, and accomplished in their fields at the time they are admitted to AMP. By all ordinary standards, they could be expected to view a course of intensive training as an obligation or a phase of their lives that has come and gone. But regardless of how they enter AMP—be it entirely voluntary or at the request of a superior—they leave with the conviction that the experience has catapulted them to a new level of competence.

Why is this so? Because the essence of the Advanced Management Program experience is ideas. The program is filled with case studies, charts, graphs, formulas, and anecdotes—the standard forms of educational content. But it is the ideas that count most. The ideas that prompt experienced executives to make changes in the way they think, act, lead, inspire, innovate, and compete. This is what I have sought to capture in the book. Based on my experience with hundreds of businesspeople in dozens of industries during various stages of their careers, I focused on the ideas that appeared to have the greatest value for achieving personal and corporate success.

Think of it as a voyage of discovery in which the insights of the senior Harvard Business School faculty are fused with the pragmatic experience of the best and brightest business leaders to produce an eclectic body of knowledge that reflects this time-tested philosophy:

He who knows the most, and continues to learn the most, wins.

A GLOBAL PERSPECTIVE—RECENT ADVANCED MANAGEMENT PROGRAM SPONSORING COMPANIES

Anglo American Corporation of South Africa
Ashland, Inc.
AT&T
Bertelsmann AG
The Boeing Company
British Airways
Chase Manhattan
Chinese Petroleum Corporation
Dana Corporation
Deutsche Bank AG
Eastman Kodak
General Motors
Hewlett-Packard
The Industrial Bank of Japan, Ltd.
Johnson & Johnson
Kaiser Foundation Health Plan
L G Group
Merrill Lynch

Mitsubishi
The Siam Cement Public Company, Ltd.
The Southern Company
TECHINT Organization
Toshiba Corporation
Unilever
Union Pacific
United Technologies

ADVANCED MANAGEMENT PROGRAM COMMANDERS

The following are among the professors who teach, or have taught, courses in the Advanced Management Program:

Michael Beer, Cahners-Rabb Professor of Business Administration, is a specialist in organizational effectiveness, managing change, and human resource management. He is chairman of the Strategic Human Resource Management program, a Harvard Executive Education program for senior human resource executives. Professor Beer is currently developing and researching a process by which a general manager can engage his organization in identifying barriers to strategy implementation and making fundamental change. His book *The Critical Path to Corporate Renewal*, a study of corporate change, won the 1991 Johnson Smith & Knisely Executive Leadership Award for best book on executive leadership. His most recent book is *Breaking the Code of Change*, edited with Nitin Nohria.

William E. Fruhan, Jr., holds the George E. Bates Professorship. He was one of the early developers of value-based management. His current research is in corporate restructuring and in developing business-level and corporate strategies to enhance shareholder value. Professor Fruhan has written four books, *Case Problems in Finance, Revitalizing Business: Shareholder/Work Force Conflicts, Financial Strategy,* and *The Fight for Competitive Advantage.* He is director of several industrial, service, and financial firms.

Robert H. Hayes is the Philip Caldwell Professor of Business Administration Emeritus. He has conducted research and course development work in Switzerland and Hong Kong on manufacturing competitiveness, technological development, and the integration of design with manufacturing. Professor Hayes has published widely, including a number of articles and six books. His latest book is *Strategic Operations: Competing Through Capabilities.* He was also a founding faculty member of Managing Global Opportunities, another Harvard Executive Education program, which focuses on exploring emerging market opportunities around the world.

Jay O. Light, the Dwight P. Robinson, Jr., Professor of Business Administration, is a graduate of Cornell University (Engineering Physics) and Harvard University (the joint doctoral program in Decision and Control). He worked in data communications at Bell Labs, in satellite guidance at the Jet Propulsion Laboratory, in management consulting at Boston Consulting Group, and in investment research with a small hedge fund before joining the faculty of the Harvard Business School in 1970. On a leave of absence from Harvard from 1977 to 1979, he was the Director of Investment and Financial Policies for the Ford Foundation. He has taught investment management, capital markets, and is currently teaching entrepreneurial finance in the second year of the MBA program. He teaches in various executive programs for CFOs and general managers. Professor Light has written *The Financial System* and numerous articles and case studies. His research and course development interests include risk management for global investment management, negotiation and deal structuring in private equity markets, and financing new technology ventures.

F. Warren McFarlan, the Albert H. Gordon Professor of Business Administration, conducts research on how information technology is transforming channels of distribution, organization structure, and service levels. A particular focus is on the steps management needs to take to ensure success, with a particular emphasis on outsourcing issues. His most recent book is *Corporate Information Systems Management: The Issues Facing Senior Executives,* 5th edition. His article "Working on Nonprofit Boards: Don't Assume the Shoe Fits" appeared in the *Harvard Business Review* November-December 1999 issue.

W. Earl Sasser, the UPS Foundation Professor of Service Management, Senior Associate Dean of Executive Education, is a pioneer in the field of service management, offering the first course research on the topic of how organizations achieve breakthrough service. His most recent books are *The Service Profit Chain* (with HBS Professor James L. Heskett and Leonard A. Schlesinger) and *Service Breakthroughs: Changing the Rules of the Game.* Sasser has chaired the MBA and the Advance Management Program.

Hugo Uyterhoeven, the Timken Professor of Business

Administration Emeritus, received doctor of law degrees from the University of Zurich in Switzerland and from the University of Ghent in Belgium and the MBA and DBA degrees from Harvard University. As a member of the Harvard Business School faculty, he has taught courses in business policy, business government and the international economy, industry and competitive analysis, management of international business, competition and strategy, and the general manager's perspective. He has taught extensively in the school's executive education programs and has served as chairman of the Advanced Management Program.

Richard H. K. Vietor, Senior John Heinz Professor of Environmental Management, teaches courses in international political economy, the regulation of business, and environmental management. He is the author of articles, case studies, and six books on various aspects of government regulation. Among these are *Energy Policy in America* and *Contrived Competition and Business Management and the National Environment.*

David F. Yoffie, the Max and Doris Starr Professor of International Business Administration, focuses his research and consulting on competitive strategy and international competition. His current research focuses on the Internet and e-commerce. Professor Yoffie has written for such publications as the *New York Times* and *Wall Street Journal.* In addition, he has written numerous books, including *Competing in the Age of Digital Convergence* and *Competing on Internet Time: Lessons from Netscape and Its Battle with Microsoft,* which was named one of the top ten business books of 1998 by *Business Week* and Amazon.com.

SOURCES

Beer, Michael and Gregory C. Rogers, "Human Resources at Hewlett-Packard," Harvard Business School Case, November 1, 1995 (Document 495-051).

Berg, Norman A., "The Lincoln Electric Co.," *Civil Engineering*, January 1973.

Berg, Norman A. and Norman D. Fast, "The Lincoln Electric Co.," Harvard Business School Case, July 29, 1983 (Document 376-028).

Bradach, Jeffrey, "Organizational Alignment: The 7-S Model," Harvard Business School Note, November 19, 1996 (Document 497-045).

Browne, John and Steven E. Prokesch, "Unleashing the Power of Learning: An Interview with BP's John Browne," *Harvard Business Review,* September-October 1997.

Collins, James C. and Jerry I. Porras, "Building Your

167

Company's Vision," *Harvard Business Review,* September-October 1996.

"The Company Behind the Image," *Forbes,* November 27, 1989, pp. 89, 92.

Cruikshank, Jeffrey, *A Delicate Experiment: The Harvard Business School 1908–1945,* Boston: Harvard Business School Press, 1987.

"Grill-to-Grill with Japan," *Business Week* (Special Issue on Quality), January 1991, p. 39.

"Here Come the Hot New Luxury Cars," *Fortune,* July 2, 1990, p. 60.

Heskett, James L., Thomas O. Jones, Gary W. Loveman, W. Earl Sasser, Jr., and Leonard A. Schlesinger, "Putting the Service Profit Chain to Work," *Harvard Business Review,* March-April 1994.

Hill, Linda A., "A Note for Analyzing Work Groups," Harvard Business School Note, April 3, 1998 (Document 496-026).

Hollenbeck, George P., "What Did You Learn in School? Studies of a University Executive Program," *Human Resource Planning,* vol. 14, no. 4, 1991, pp. 249–51.

Jones, Thomas O. and W. Earl Sasser, Jr., "Why Satisfied Customers Defect," *Harvard Business Review,* November-December 1995.

Kotter, John, *A Force for Change,* New York: Free Press, 1990.

Leonard-Barton, Dorothy, "Core Capabilities and Core Rigidities: A Paradox in Managing New Product Development," *Strategic Management Journal,* 1992.

Nohria, Nitin, "Note on Organizational Structure," Harvard Business School Note, June 30, 1995 (Document 491-083).

Pfeffer, Jeffrey, *Competitive Advantage Through People,* Boston: Harvard Business School Press, 1994.

Piper, Thomas R., "Clarkson Lumber Co.," Harvard Business School Case, October 29, 1996 (Document 297-028).

Porter, Michael E., "How Competitive Forces Shape Strategy," *Harvard Business Review,* March-April 1979, pp. 143–44.

Porter, Michael E., "What Is Strategy?" *Harvard Business Review,* November-December 1996.

Quinn, Judy, "The Welch Way: General Electric CEO Jack Welch Brings Employee Empowerment to Light," *Incentive,* September 1994.

Sewell, Carl, Paul P. Brown, and Tom Peters, *Customers for Life: How to Turn that One-Time Buyer into a Lifetime Customer,* New York: Pocket Books, 1998.

Tichy, Noel M. and Stratford Sherman, *Control Your Destiny or Someone Else Will: How Jack Welch Is Making General Electric the World's Most Competitive Corporation,* New York: Currency/Doubleday, 1993.

Waterman, R.H., T.J. Peters, and J.R. Phillips, "Structure Is Not Organization," *Business Horizons,* June 1980, pp. 14–26.

Welch, Jack, "Walking the Talk at GE," *Training and Development,* June 1993, p. 30.

Wheelwright, Steven C. and Robert H. Hayes, "Competing Through Manufacturing," *Harvard Business Review,* January-February 1985, pp. 103, 106–9.

INDEX